KT-211-012

'Irreverent, inspiring and engaging. Humour and wisdom drip from every page. If you're a boring academic look away now. The rest of you read on. You won't be disappointed. Promise.'

Paul McGee

'Practical insights on how to make positive thinking work for you. And without any of the pastel-coloured, muzak-themed humourless preachy-ness that so often makes you give up on this useful and important topic.'

*Michael Bungay Stanier, author of **Do More Great Work***

'The *Brilliant* philosophy is simple, funny, profound and it gets results. The two Andy's wonderful down-to-earth book appeals to my no nonsense northern outlook with great practical ideas you can immediately apply both at home and work.'

*Steve McDermott, European motivational speaker of the year and best-selling author of **How To Be a Complete and Utter Failure In Life, Work and Everything***

'Fun & thought provoking. Love it!'

*Andy Gilbert, author and creator of the **Go MAD Thinking System***

'Life's too short folks. We all need a reminder that positive attitudes get positive results so follow the simple advice, be your best self and stand tall.'

Diana Higman, Medallist at World Transplant Games

'*The Art of Being Brilliant* has been a major contributing factor to our successes in maximising happiness and creating our world beating team. Deciding to be BRILLIANT can and will change your life for the better!'

Rick Turner, Businessman, entrepreneur and theme park owner, www.thebigsheep.co.uk

'If you're informationed out (like me) and just want a result...congratulations... here it is.'

Richard Wilkins, UK Minister of Inspiration, www.theministryofinspiration.com

'Chin up, chin up. Everyone loves a happy face. Wear it. Have it. It'll brighten the darkest place. Twinkle. Sparkle. Let a little sunshine in. You'll be on the right side looking on the bright side. Up with your chinny-chin-chin.'

E. B. White, Charlotte's Web, *1952*

THE ART OF BEING BRILLIANT

Transform your life by doing what works for you

Andy Cope and Andy Whittaker
Illustrations by Laura E Martin

CAPSTONE

© 2012 Andy Cope and Andy Whittaker

Registered office
Capstone Publishing Ltd. (A Wiley Company), John Wiley and Sons Ltd, The Atrium, Southern Gate, Chichester, West Sussex, PO19 8SQ, United Kingdom

David J. Pollay's *The Law of the Garbage Truck*® was used with permission by Sterling Publishing Co., Inc. Copyright © 2004-2010 by David J. Pollay.

The Law of the Garbage Truck is a registered ® trademark of David J. Pollay

For details of our global editorial offices, for customer services and for information about how to apply for permission to reuse the copyright material in this book please see our website at www.wiley.com.

Wiley publishes in a variety of print and electronic formats and by print-on-demand. Some material included with standard print versions of this book may not be included in e-books or in print-on-demand. If this book refers to media such as a CD or DVD that is not included in the version you purchased, you may download this material at http://booksupport.wiley.com. For more information about Wiley products, visit www.wiley.com.

Designations used by companies to distinguish their products are often claimed as trademarks. All brand names and product names used in this book are trade names, service marks, trademarks or registered trademarks of their respective owners. The publisher is not associated with any product or vendor mentioned in this book. This publication is designed to provide accurate and authoritative information in regard to the subject matter covered. It is sold on the understanding that the publisher is not engaged in rendering professional services. If professional advice or other expert assistance is required, the services of a competent professional should be sought.

Library of Congress Cataloging-in-Publication Data is available.

A catalogue record for this book is available from the British Library.

ISBN 978-0-857-08371-5 (pbk) ISBN 978-0-857-08374-6 (ebk)
ISBN 978-0-857-08373-9 (ebk) ISBN 978-0-857-08372-2 (ebk)

Designed by Andy Prior Design
Printed in Great Britain by TJ International Ltd, Padstow, Cornwall, UK

For Ed Peppitt, without whose vision and enthusiasm this book would never have seen the light of day. Ed, we're truly grateful.

CONTENTS LIST

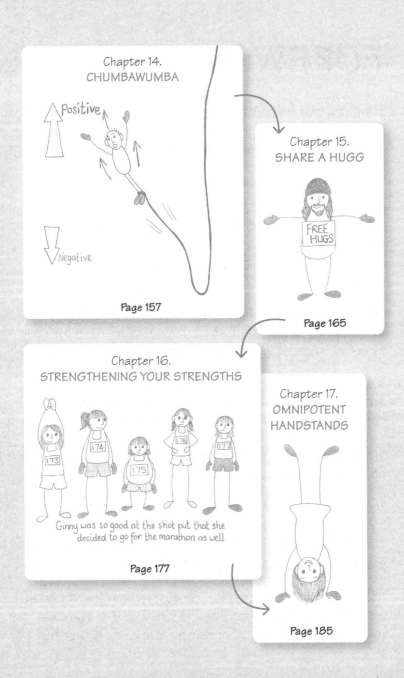

FOREWORD

Have you ever achieved something in your life that you are very proud of, and then someone else comes along and does it better, like being trumped at cards?

Well, there I was, thinking I had achieved that elusive magic element in 'The Naked Leader' books – simplicity. Simplicity in stripping down to the essentials, and then stripping them down even further, until you end up with pure common sense, which in this age of information overwhelm is, sadly, not so common.

Then along came Andy Cope's first book, *Being Brilliant*. Full of the blindingly obvious, stuff we can make happen in our personal as well as business lives, and with bags of humour thrown in.

And, to add insult to injury, he even had the bare-faced cheek to ask me for an endorsement! How was I supposed to endorse a book that does what I set out to do, but so much better?

Still, I wrote an endorsement, consoled myself that this was a one off, a true one book wonder, and relaxed.

Then one day – THUMP – a large envelope hit the mat. And, guess what? It was now two Andys with this book – *The Art of Being Brilliant*. And this time they didn't just want an endorsement, they wanted me to write a foreword!

No way. How am I supposed to write about a book that is written with such easy-to-follow language, in such a clear and practical style, and which has at least one simple idea on every page that you can make happen straight away?

And with illustrations!!

No, it's all too much.

Sorry Andys – the answer has to be no.

Now, will you please stop writing such great books, and go get proper jobs!

David Taylor

David works with world-class leaders and organisations, is author of the best-selling 'Naked Leader' books, the Honorary Professor of Leadership at Warwick University Business School and a Business Ambassador for The Prince's Trust. www.nakedleader.com

JIMMY'S DIARY

He hadn't been up there for years. Probably decades! In the faint light of the attic, the old man shuffled across to a pile of boxes that lay near one of the cobwebbed windows. Brushing aside the dust, he began to lift out one old photo album after another.

His search began with the fond recollection of the love of his life – long gone. He knew that somewhere in these albums was the photo he was looking for. It was the black-and-white one, when she had that smile. Patiently opening the long lost treasures he was soon lost in a sea of memories. The old man wiped away one or two happy tears. Although the world had not stopped spinning when his wife left it, the past was more alive than his present emptiness.

Setting aside one of the dusty albums, he pulled from the box what appeared to be a diary from his son's childhood. He couldn't recall ever having seen it before – or even the fact that his son had kept a diary. Opening the yellowed pages, he glanced over the entries and his lips turned up at the corners in an unconscious smile. His eyes shone and he chuckled aloud. He realized he wasn't just reading the words, he could hear them, spoken by his young son who'd grown up far too fast in that very house. In the utter silence of the attic, the earnest words of a six-year-old worked their magic and the old man was carried back to a time almost forgotten. The spidery handwriting reflected on important issues for a six-year-old – school, football, holidays, arguments with his big sister – entry after entry stirred a sentimental hunger in the old man's heart. But it was accompanied by a painful memory that his son's simple recollections of those days didn't tally with his own. The old man's wrinkles became more deeply etched.

He remembered that he'd kept a business diary. He closed his son's journal and turned to leave, having forgotten the cherished photo that had triggered his initial search. Hunched over to keep from bumping his head on the beams, the old man stepped down the wooden stairway to his office. He wasn't sure what creaked most, the stairs or his knees!

He opened a glass cabinet door, reached in and sought his business diary. He placed the journals side by side. His was leather bound, his name embossed in gold. His son's was tatty and frayed with a hand-drawn picture on the front. The old man ran a bony finger across the name 'Jimmy' scribbled on the cover.

He opened his business journal and read some of the entries. There were notes from meetings, often very detailed. Every single day had been crammed with business appointments. Sometimes the evenings too. He remembered back to those times... he sure was driven in his career. It was for the love of his family that he'd chased success so hard. The old man was drawn to an entry much shorter than the rest. In his own neat handwriting were these words, 'Wasted a whole day fishing with Jimmy. Didn't catch a thing!'

With a deep sigh and a shaking hand he took Jimmy's journal and found the boy's entry for the same day, 4 June. Large scrawling letters pressed deep into the paper read, 'Went fishing with my dad. Best day of my life.'

'Many men go fishing all of their lives without knowing that it is not fish they are after.'

Henry David Thoreau

Chapter 1
FISHING FOR LIFE

In which we finally get the point of fishing! We find out we already have all the answers, discover happiness isn't for sale and that it's certainly not 'out there'. We peep at academic porn and get a cool quote from Groucho Marx.

Andy W and I have been working for numerous years as personal development trainers in businesses and schools. We've covered bread-and-butter topics that all trainers worth their salt should be able to deliver. You know, subjects such as communication, leadership, conflict resolution, assertiveness, coaching skills, goal setting, teams… blah, blah, blah. But recently we've discovered something new. Well 'new' might be a bit strong, but certainly 'different'. We've blended some of the more modern concepts and hot topics into a workshop that we boldly call 'The Art of Being Brilliant'. And, do you know what? It really works!

What do you think about the story of Jimmy's Diary? How did it make you think and feel? Because our aim is to get you to think and feel very differently. To realise what's important in life. And to make changes where necessary.

We are both very excited about the future. In fact Andy and I have got a lot in common. You're bright so will have cottoned on to the fact that we're both called 'Andy'. We've both worked all over the world. We're both dads. We're both 'self help junkies', having read every personal development book that's ever been published. We laugh at the same things. We're both devilishly young and good looking. We're both prone to exaggeration…

You get the picture. Most importantly, we share a philosophy and a common outlook on how training should be. It has become very clear to us over the last couple of years that the people we work with already know everything there is to know about creating a happy and successful life. Everyone has all the resources they need. How exciting is that? You already have all the answers! It's just that the majority of people have lost touch with them. Or forgotten them. And the result is that we hit peaks of happiness and positivity on an ad hoc basis. We feel 'brilliant' sporadically. Sometimes quite by accident – because we're waiting for the right conditions. Maybe a holiday will make us happy. Or a new shirt. Or a car. Or a few beers?

The problem is that most people are looking in the wrong place. Richard Wilkins (http://www.theministryofinspiration. com) describes it brilliantly when he talks of people searching for happiness, fulfilment and positive feelings in the filing cabinet marked 'external'. Happiness is 'out there' somewhere.

You should listen to Richard – after all, he is the UK's self-styled 'Minister of Inspiration' and, to be honest, you've got to have some guts to give yourself that title. Many 'gurus' fail to live up to their own hype. Richard sets his hype very high and clears the bar with ease. The man is brilliant.

So we agree with Richard – we believe that most people are looking for happiness and fulfilment in the wrong filing cabinet. We think you should check out the filing cabinet marked 'internal'. All the great feelings you ever experienced are already inside you!

> 'The future's so bright, I gotta wear shades.'
>
> *Pat MacDonald, songwriter of the 1986 hit for Timbuk3*

So our job has become easy. We don't have to teach people anything. All we have to do is devise a cunning way of reconnecting people with their own internal resources, putting them in touch with information which has been buried in their unconscious mind. Or, to keep it simple, get them to look in the right filing cabinet, the one marked 'internal'.

Oh, and this book is the key!

I used to teach on MBA programmes. Boy, did I work hard. I would roll up my sleeves and get stuck into Maslow, Herzberg and maybe throw in a dash of 'situational leadership'. Oh, and let's not forget the tried and trusted Belbin and Myers Briggs.

Who cares if they've covered it a dozen times before? Bring on the self perception questionnaire – you might have changed since last time! I was happiest when scribing interlocking circle diagrams on a flipchart. Or maybe drawing a pyramid. I used to call it 'academic pornography'. A real turn on for managers.

Except it wasn't. You see, the penny's dropped. Theories have their place. In fact, hats off to those clever boffins who come up with interlocking circles and sexy new acronyms (I feel SMART needs a rebrand though, it's gone way past its sell-by date). The problem with traditional management training is that life isn't a theory. It's very, very practical.

And relentless – it just keeps coming at us. In fact, let's face it, for most people, life is exhausting. The morbid obesity of change is weighing us down. So we've come to the conclusion that the world doesn't need any more complex theories.

> 'A child of five would understand this.
> Send someone to fetch a child of five.'
> *Groucho Marx*

We need stuff that works. The simpler the better. We need to reconnect with what's important. Not in a Buddhist[1], inner peace, tofu-eating way – more of an upgrade-of-the-software-between-our-ears kind of way. This book is crammed full of common sense. The trouble is, it certainly isn't common practice!

So Andy W and I have pooled the best bits of what we know. There are a few case studies, some funny stuff and some questions to make you think about your work, relationships and life. There is plenty of academia behind it, but we've weeded out the nonsense and debunked the academic porn. Without you knowing it, we'll be sneaking in concepts such as 'Positive Psychology', 'Appreciative Inquiry', 'Neuro Linguistic Programming' and 'Emotional Intelligence'. We like to think of the book as an intellectual smoothie – a blend of the best ingredients, with the pith removed!

The Art of Being Brilliant is designed around half a dozen commonsense principles – we call them the 'super six'. The book's also designed to make you think. Maybe even to make you laugh. But the underlying message is deadly serious. We're talking about you and your life. Read it. Do it. The results will reverberate positively at work and at home. It's become abundantly clear to us that 'success' isn't about becoming a

---

[1] *Other religions are available.*

different person. It's a matter of finding out what really works for you, and doing more of it!

The reality is that life is too short. Why settle for being anything less than yourself, brilliantly?

'He who
laughs, lasts.'

Mary Poole

Chapter 2

SHINY HAPPY PEOPLE

In which we come clean about Positive Psychology,
we find out why Britain fails to qualify for the
'Happiness World Cup', a blissful picture is painted,
Woody Allen tries to depress us and we're introduced
to mood hoovers and 2%ers.

We've been advocates of the relatively new field of positive psychology since its inception in the late 1990s. I've been so enthused about it myself that I'm doing a doctorate on it! Psychology was part and parcel of my first degree. I read numerous academic tomes on depression, anxiety, eating disorders, phobias…and became an expert on all things negative! In fact, it was quite depressing studying it!

Interestingly, I was recently asked to do a talk at an NHS conference. The theme of the conference was mental health and wellbeing. Right up my street, so I agreed and they slotted me in as the final speaker on Day 3. A few days before the conference I received the agenda and it wasn't about health and wellbeing at all! To give you a flavour, the speakers on Day 1 were talking about suicide rates in Bridgend and depression amongst social workers. Day 2 started with a corker, Prozac addiction, before moving on to sleeping disorders and the rise of youth crime. My supposedly uplifting talk, called 'The Art of Being Brilliant', had been slotted in after 'Exponential Anorexia'.

My heart sank! Such a snappy title! How could I follow that?

The entire conference was devoted to mental ill-health and feeling grim. It was homing in on what was going wrong and, to be frank, it's typical of the world of research and medicine. I'm not suggesting it's wrong to have conferences about such subjects. I'm suggesting it's normal. We've spent billions of pounds producing pills to cure depression but it seems to be getting worse!

Strap yourself in, because I feel compelled to give you the science bit. Traditional strands of psychology were couched in terms of the study of ill people. We'd spent hundreds of years studying what was wrong with people. In a nutshell, you'd only ever go and see a psychologist if you were ill. You'd never book yourself in for an appointment if you were feeling great!

'Positive psychology' has existed formally since the late 1980s. Its popularity mushroomed with the publication of Dr Martin Seligman's book, *Authentic Happiness* in 2003. However, even the good Doctor wouldn't claim to have invented 'positivity' and 'happiness' – they've been on the radar for centuries! Check out Plato and Confucius for a start. Or the big fella they call Buddha. And more recently Carl Rogers, Richard Bandura, Howard Gardiner and the God of management courses the world over, Abe Maslow (if I hear his 'hierarchy of needs' trotted out on any more courses I'll scream and scream until I'm sick). All have elements of self-fulfilment, happiness and efficacy in their studies. So it's hitting today's headlines but I guess positive psychology is best described as having a short history with a very long past.

There's a general acknowledgement that psychology has followed a 'disease model'. Basically, if individuals lie on a range of wellbeing from -10 (very unwell) to +10 (very well indeed) then we've always been focused on getting people from, say, -7 to zero (to the point of them 'not being ill'). Job done! Except, of course, it isn't! Because, you see, there's a huge difference between 'being alive' and 'living'.

Positive psychology is about getting to +8 or +9. The best word I can find to describe this is 'flourishing' and it's firmly established at the 'living' end of the spectrum.

So, positive psychology hasn't invented happiness and wellbeing, merely brought it under one umbrella. It's been a re-focusing exercise rather than a revolution (although we're rather excited by it and would therefore like to whip you up into a frenzy of enthusiasm thereby leading to a revolution…more of that later).

Brenda was delighted to have discovered what STRESSED was when spelt backwards

Quite a lot of the 'remedies' for getting people to be happier seem intuitively obvious. Maybe even simplistic. We feel this may be a problem in terms of getting people to take the subject seriously. There's certainly a lot of scepticism out there. Tabloids like to belittle it with headlines such as 'happyology' or by pouring scorn on positive psychology in schools as 'attempts to teach teens to be happy!' (When, of course, we should be teaching them something really useful like algebra or ox-bow lakes.)

And herein lies one of the major hurdles for the subject. 'Happiness' seems to be a collective term for a range of emotions. It's subjective (which has led to the term 'subjective wellbeing', the theme of several major studies by the heavyweight academic community). It's difficult to measure because how do we gauge 'happiness' on a scale of 1–10? And what causes happiness in one person may not cause it in another.

And another question worth pondering is why bother studying 'happiness' and 'positivity' at all? Hasn't the research community got better things to do than tell us what we already know? I think it's worth spending a couple of lines on the benefits of positive psychology (just in case the penny hasn't dropped yet). It seems an obvious point but, basically, emotion drives motion (i.e., the way you feel drives your behaviour).

Here are some of Jessica Pryce-Jones's (2010) business stats about happy people:

- They get promoted faster
- They have 180% more energy
- They are 108% more engaged in their job
- They achieve more
- They are 40% more confident
- They give better customer service
- They are more creative

I could go on, but I think it's fairly obvious that these are the kind of people you need in your organisation.[2]

But the benefits spread wider than the workplace. On a societal level, happy people live longer, have fewer ailments, are more altruistic, have more friends and make other people feel great too!

---

[2] I used to know a manager who presided over a very dour team. He described himself as 'chairman of the bored'. And I'm still chuckling 14 years later.

At a family level, positive psychology encourages flourishing families. A bit clichéd but true, families that play together stay together. Once again, it seems an obvious point but positive parents tend to produce positive offspring. Is there a more important role that you'll ever play?

There are even international happiness league tables! Countries are rated according to health service, education, job market, infrastructure and such like, to come up with a happiness score. I was intrigued to find out whether there was a link between happiness and income. It's true that very poor people will feel happier if they receive more income. But once you've got food in your tum, a roof over your head and enough to pay the bills, more money won't increase your happiness levels. Having said that, there is a nifty way of squeezing extra value from your happiness pound – buy an experience rather than a product. So, for example, a trip to the seaside will yield more happiness Brownie points than a new pair of shoes.

Will a lottery win make you happier? This is counter-intuitive but the short answer is 'No'! Several studies of lottery winners have found there is a spike of happiness but that they returned to their pre-win level after a few months. Scientifically, this is called 'habituation' and it means we soon become accustomed to our situation and it ceases to bring happiness. It's the same with a pay rise – the initial increase will be brilliant but the effect wears off as we get used to the change (unless, of course, you spend it entirely on trips to the seaside!).

We are obsessed with measures of economic success. The news tells us that the FTSE is up 26 points or the Dow has fallen. Or the pound is up against the euro. And the Hang Seng has reacted badly to factory output data in Shanghai. Or that 'America has sneezed and we've caught a cold'. The papers have financial pages with reams of company data. It seems our indicators of 'success' are purely financial.

If we scratch the surface of this just for a second, we'll find that national income goes up every time there's a car crash or a divorce. Or after a flood. And, brilliant news, GDP shoots up in times of war. I can imagine the UK government hatching a strategy to cope with the recession…invade France (again!).

'We're measuring just about everything except that which makes us happy.'

Unknown

So, that begs the question, are we measuring the right things? Should we, in fact, be measuring happiness?

Looking internationally, it's interesting that 'Happiness' appears in the American Declaration of Independence. Well, the pursuit of happiness actually. (So in America you have a right to chase it but never quite get there!) Closer to home, Denmark consistently ranks as the happiest nation in Europe. I did a fact-finding tour of Costa Rica, one of the world's happiest countries, and can safely report that they're poor, they don't have an army, it rains every day, there are huge holes in the road…and they're happy! Bhutan (a small and, by material standards, very poor country in the Himalayas) measures 'Gross Domestic Happiness'. So, for them, 'success' isn't about churning goods out of their factories; it's about creating an infrastructure that enables their citizens to flourish.

The UK government has recently initiated a national happiness survey, much to the chagrin of the popular press. 'Waste of Money' screamed the *Express*. 'Happy Clappy Nonsense', suggested a *Mail* columnist. (The irony that a happiness survey has created so much anger seems to have been lost on everyone but me.)

> 'Wealth is what you have left over when all your money's run out.'
>
> Roger Hamilton

But, you see, the answers to deep-rooted questions about happiness and positivity may be simple, but they're not easy. We will reveal the 'secrets' of happiness and positivity in this book and you'll roll your eyes and think, 'I already knew that!' And herein lies the conundrum: if we already know the answers, why aren't we happier?

Anecdotally, we all know a few really happy and upbeat people (although if you think about it, it's actually very few). But because they're not a drain on society – hardly ever ill, don't go to the docs, just kind of get on with life in a positive, energetic way – we've never really bothered about them. Dr Martin Seligman woke us up. Who the hell are these happy people? Why are they so damned happy? And, crucially, what can we learn from them that we can put into practice so we can join them? Good gracious, this is heady stuff. I can see why I wanted to learn more. I wanted to be one of them!

Andy W's take on this is similar but, as usual, much funnier. Psychology has always been focused on, and concerned with, fixing people. It's been the study of problems. Someone would walk into the psychologist's surgery and the doctor would ask them to lie on the couch. The doctor would sit at one end with his/her note pad and pen and then say, 'What's the problem?' The patient would then unleash all of their worldly issues. The doctor would then say, 'Is there anything else I can help you with?' and the person would then find even more issues and so the process went on. Some people have been in therapy for years, spending their hard-earned cash lying on a couch telling a stranger about their problems. It's big business! We have been studying what's wrong with people for centuries; there must be warehouses full of boxes stuffed with people's problems. The point is that the focus was always on the problem(s).

Seligman re-focused the research. He started to examine what was right with people. There are people in the world who wake up in a morning, spring out of bed and say, 'Yippee, I'm alive!' They look across at their bed to find their perfect partner lying there, they then open the curtains in their beautiful home to hear the birds singing. The sun is shining. They put on their silk dressing gown and fluffy slippers and make their way downstairs to find their perfect children lined up at the breakfast bar.

> 'Remember we're all winners. Out of all those millions of sperm you got there first. Rejoice!'
>
> *Paul McGee*

'Morning Father/Mother,' they say.
'Morning children,' beams the parent. 'How's school?'
'Wonderful. Straight As,' they all reply.

They then get dressed and walk to their big double garage which they open to find themselves faced with the dilemma of whether to take the Ferrari or the Bentley. They think to themselves, 'Bugger it, I will walk. I don't need to be in the office until lunch time anyway.' They then walk down their big driveway, crunching on the gravel, waving at the gardener, with a big smile on their face. They whistle with joy as the badgers and foxes cavort at their feet and birds land on their shoulders…

OK, so the passage above may be a tad exaggerated. But the wider point remains valid. Who are these happy people? Are they rich? Or are they just like you and I?

Until recently, we didn't know, because 'happiness' wasn't on the science radar. Nobody ever went to a psychologist, knocked on the door and said, 'I have a big house, loads of money, a great

Thought I'd better come and tell you how fab I've been feeling!

career, perfect partner and kids. I'm so happy I think I'm going to burst. For God's sake, please help me!' For some reason it just didn't happen.

> 'It's life, Jim. But not as we know it.'
>
> *Mis-quote, often attributed to Bones McCoy, Star Trek[3]*

I have sought out these 'happy people'. Interesting that I felt the need to put that in inverted commas, as if 'happy people' means something slightly odd. 'Happy people.' Oh, yes, we know what you mean Andy. 'Weirdoes. Cloud Cuckoo land. Ga ga.' There is even a case being made to include 'Happiness' in that big book, the Diagnostic and Statistical Manual of Mental Disorders on account of its rarity. It's true!

Breathe easy. Happy people aren't nutters and they don't live in the rarefied atmosphere of Walton Mountain. The remainder of this book is spent telling you the 'secrets' of happiness and positivity. We have sought out research into positive people as well as the positive people themselves. It's been written up in my thesis, all 80,000 words of it. And, because it's a doctorate, I've had to try and make them big, complicated words! But if you lose the academic clap-trap, you're left with some clear, simple and do-able principles.

The following diagram sums it up. The great news is that happy people are as sane as you or I (well, you at least). We refer to them as the top 2%ers.

---

[3] *Dr McCoy never actually said this! And, believe it or not, the line 'Beam me up, Scotty' was never heard on Star Trek either!*

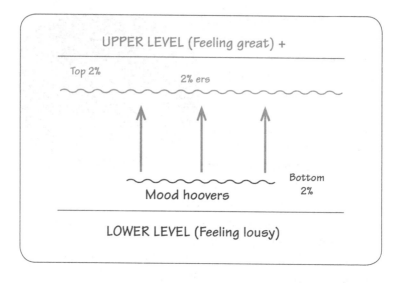

This represents a graph of your wellbeing (your 'feelings', for want of a simpler word). The straight black lines represent your upper and lower levels of 'feel good' factor. So, on a normal day, you will live your life between these two limits of top end 'feel good' and bottom end 'feel lousy'. You already knew that. You can feel great or feel rubbish. Some people can get stuck in the bottom section. They are not clinically depressed, just stuck in a cycle of negativity. These are doom and gloom merchants who love to whinge about things. Any topic will do. We call them 'mood hoovers'.

'Mood hoover' definitions and/or descriptions:
'Someone who has a problem for every solution.'
Or, 'Every silver lining has a cloud.'

Or, classically, 'If there are two people talking and one looks bored, he's the other one.'

Henry from accounts just didn't get the irony

I'm trying to add a modicum of humour but there's not really much to laugh about. Mood hoovers suck all the energy out of you, leaving you feeling as rubbish as they do. It doesn't take many mood hoovers to drag down a team. We've seen it happen in whole organisations where the culture is stuck in permanent negativity. We've met teachers who are mood hoovers (rather too many if we're absolutely honest). And accountants. And police officers. Even professional footballers! We've met public sector, private sector and charity sector mood hoovers. Rich ones, poor ones, fat ones, thin ones, black ones and white ones (but not many gay ones, strangely. Maybe the original meaning of 'gay' stuck for a reason?)

So, it seems that negative people are drawn from almost all walks of life. The big problem in businesses is if it's the managers who are the mood hoovers![4]

---

[4] Note to self, that's another book for another day.

Back to the diagram. There's a swathe of people in the middle section. They visit the real highs and lows but spend most of their time occupying the middle ground. Their moods tend to be determined by what happens to them during the day. These are ordinary people who have loads of ordinary days. Most of the time they're 'fine'. We have no axe to grind with these people, but we're certain that they can learn things that will enable them to raise their game. If you've only got one go at life then 'fine' seems a little tame.[5]

> 'If my films make one more person miserable, I'll feel I have done my job.'
> *Woody Allen*

And, last but by no means least, there are the top 2%ers. These are people who are consistently upbeat and positive (not all day every day, but are habitually more inclined to be positive). Life can throw them some awful circumstances but they seem to thrive. They are solution-focused, energetic and can-do. They tend to get things done (while the mood hoovers roll their eyes and moan that they can't be done) and, crucially, they raise the levels of optimism and energy in those around them. In short, they're good to have around – at work and at home!

This book is about the top 2%ers. They're not rich and famous. They don't drive Ferraris. But they are happy! So, think about it, do you know a top 2%er?

Yes you do. Here's some good news. You are one!

Think back to the last time you had a brilliant day. A day when

---

[5] *We decided against calling this book The Art of Being Mediocre. There didn't seem much point.*

you felt like you could take on the world. Think about all the good feelings you had. Invincibility, happiness, joy, positivity, energy, passion... you were being a 2%er. The truth is that we all visit these fantastic times on a random basis. But what if we could learn to feel like that more often? What if we could learn some simple principles so that feeling great became a habit?

More good news. You can! It's dead simple. Andy W is originally from Morecambe (recently voted the 3rd worst place to live in Britain) and now lives in Mansfield (recently voted the 2nd worst place to live in Britain). So, if he can grasp it, there's hope for us all! With a little effort and a 'can do' attitude you can achieve your dreams, create positive relationships, have more energy and have the life you want. Sure, things sometimes don't always work out as planned. To coin a phrase, 'shit happens'. Even the top 2%ers have bad days. Sometimes we need to pick ourselves back up after a knock but that's what makes life what it is – fun, exciting and challenging.

The difference between you at the bottom and you at the top of the arrow is life-changing. Our promise is that you will have a happier, more rewarding life if you live it as a top 2%er. Your relationships will be easier, life will be more fun, you'll smile more and the chances are, you'll live longer!

Andy and I have worked out that the top 2%ers have six things in common. If you want to know what they are, read on...

'I don't believe it.
Prove it to me
and I still won't
believe it.'

Douglas Adams, *Life, the Universe,
and Everything, (1982)*

Chapter 3

SOME OF THE PEOPLE, SOME OF THE TIME

In which we count down to death, get addicted to bad news and curse the dastardly British summer. Michelle has a baby and we learn why positive thinking has such a bad name. Oh, and we sneak in the most unacademic phrase in the world ever... 'willy nilly'!

It was Benjamin Disraeli who originally said, 'Lies, damn lies and statistics'. Apparently 86.72% of all statistics are made up on the spot. And you can twist statistics to make anything seem true. Here's one. Fact: men with pierced ears make better husbands.[6]

Our purpose is not to marinate you in data or drown you in statistics. Rather, our aim is to simplify the theories and bring them to you in a no-nonsense manner. Big words are great but they've never changed my life. Simple things that I can actually put into practice have changed my life. So, please excuse the simplicity of what's about to come. It's deliberate.

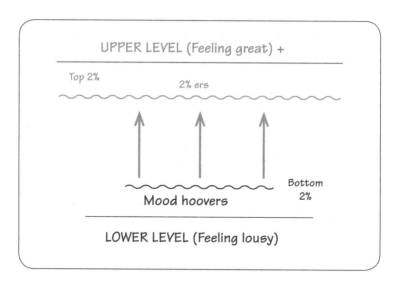

Let's go back to the diagram again. Most people nestle comfortably in the bottom third. There's a set of invisible forces, dragging us down. We count down to Friday in what Robert Holden (2005) calls 'destination addiction'. We're eager to hurry

---

[6] Probably because they've bought jewellery AND experienced pain!

life along, towards something good that lies in the future. The end of the day or the weekend. Or you might have a holiday booked in three weeks and someone asks you how you are… 'Only three weeks to go!' If you know a teacher, they will be able to tell you exactly how many days until the next half term (some can tell you the hours and minutes, sadly).

Let me make this abundantly clear: none of us has enough weeks left on this planet to count them down, wishing them away!

I call it 'stinking thinking'.

I mean, hey, we even call ourselves the 'human race'! How fast can we live it? We're always on the go. There aren't enough hours in the day. 'Busyness' has even become a mantra for success. To the typical greeting of 'How are you?' we now reply, 'Oh, you know, keeping busy.'

It's worth taking a moment to think how faulty our thinking is. If life is a race, I don't want to be first over the finishing line. And here's an interesting thought, what if the real winner of the 'human race' is the one who comes in last? Me? I'd much rather hang back and milk it a bit. Maybe put a big grin on my face as I wave to the crowd. And I'd walk the last bend, enjoying every moment.

And it's this different perspective that gets you a much better result. What if your aim wasn't merely to 'survive the week' (because the more you think about that the more ridiculous it becomes). What if your aim was to enjoy the week? Or what if your primary reason for getting out of bed on Monday morning was to inspire people?

We only have to switch on the news or glance at the newspaper to find permanent doom and gloom. Switch on your TV and you'll find something horrific on the news right now. Is it any wonder society is stuck in a negative rut?

I'm typing this particular paragraph on a gorgeous June day. I switched on the TV this morning and there was a huge sun in the middle of the weather forecaster's GB map. And the map was red, indicating 'even hotter than yellow'. Great news I thought. Bring it on! But at the bottom of the screen there were the words 'severe weather warning!' and a web address for an NHS Direct 'Hot Weather Helpline'. And the forecaster drew our attention to this with the cheery words, 'Anyone worried about the hot weather should log on and seek advice.'

I was amazed that anyone should be concerned enough about sunny weather to be driven to seek government advice... so curious in fact that I logged on! Just in case anyone was wondering what to do in the UK when the sun shines, here's the official government line on how to keep cool on a hot day:

1. Wear shorts (I swear this is true).

2. Drink lots of water (you couldn't make it up).

3. Stay in the shade (keep out of the sun...bonza idea!).

4. Do away with your duvet and sleep under a sheet or blanket (another belter...why didn't I think of that?).

5. Take a cold shower (thanks Government helpline...I think you've saved me from cooking in my own juices).

Phew! I don't know what I'd have done without that advice

(except wear shorts, drink lots of water, stay in the shade…).

It's no wonder that we get panicked by a spell of sunshine – the fact is that the vast majority of people are a million miles away from feeling as great as they could. Positive psychology doesn't say that the majority are depressed or sad. It's more that we're living life fast, but are we living it well? We reserve 'feeling brilliant' for short bursts when the sun's out. Or Friday nights – they're great. Or when a meeting goes well. Or it's half term and your journey to work is twenty minutes quicker because there's no traffic on the school run! Our natural habitat lies in the bottom third and we visit the 2% heights occasionally. Almost at random. We've met delegates on courses who've been in the bottom third of the diagram for decades! This doesn't make them sad or horrible people, just, as I said earlier (and I can't think of a better word), 'stuck'. Being negative has become a habit – they don't even know they're doing it.

> 'Anyone can start something new. It takes real leaders to stop something old.'
>
> Dan Rockwell (well worth a follow @leadershipfreak)

Let's give you a concrete example – my good friend Michelle. I've sought permission from Michelle to tell you this – and she remains a great chum of mine – but for the three years we shared an office, Michelle's catch-phrase was 'Nightmare!' That was pretty much it. She'd slope into the office in the morning, rolling her eyes because she had better things to do than come to work. 'How you doing today, Shell?'

'Don't ask,' she'd retort. 'Nightmare!'

Shell wasn't depressed or suicidal. Merely a bit stuck. In Shell's world the weather was always too cold, rainy, hot, windy – too something! Never brilliant. The phone would ring and she'd sigh.

'Phone's ringing again. That'll be a customer. Nightmare!'

This is how stuck Shell became. She eventually settled down and found a decent man to share her life with. They married and had a son. Michelle proudly brought the eight-week-old baby into the office so we could all grin and coo at the loveliness of her son. She cradled her little boy in her arms and I couldn't help but have a huge grin on my face. Michelle had grown up. 'Shell,' I exclaimed, beaming from ear to ear. 'You're a mum!'

'I know,' she sighed. 'Nightmare!'

Nightmare, it's going to be unbearably hot

Why didn't Shell's demeanour and language demonstrate her joy at her good fortune? It brings me back to the word 'stuck'.

It's a safe bet that you know some mood hoovers. If you bought them flowers they would grumble about having to get a vase. If they won the lottery they would grumble it wasn't a rollover. If you saved their life they would grumble they now have to carry on paying tax.

What do these simple examples tell us? That Andy and I know loads of dysfunctional people? Maybe, but more likely that we know loads of normal people. That negativity comes naturally. Why is that? What are the invisible forces pushing us down into what Alex Linley (2010) calls 'the curse of mediocrity'? We could give you a whirlwind tour of the evolution of the human species. We can argue from the viewpoint that we are pre-programmed to be negative. For 'negative' read 'cautious' and 'pessimistic'. We've evolved as a species because we're survivors. And we've survived because we've been cautious. Darwin's 'survival of the fittest' is quite closely aligned with 'survival of the most careful'. We call it 'defensive thinking'.

So, in modern society, negativity rules! We could blame the media. It's a given that if you switch on the news or pick up a paper then doom will prevail. We could point the finger at other people. The mood hoovers. You might even have married one! It's hard to feel inspired if the people around you are having a 'nightmare'. And then there's the weather and the traffic!

But, let's not pull any punches. Let me give it to you straight. The biggest reason why most people are a million miles away from feeling brilliant is that it's easier to be negative. In fact, it takes no effort whatsoever to conform to 'normal'. And if 'normal' means we gripe about the traffic and about the latest restructure at work and the economy and the state of the national sports teams and the weather, then so be it. We like to fit in. It's so easy to be negative and focus on all the bad stuff in the world.

> 'Start every day off with a smile and get it over with.'
> W. C. Fields, US comedian

Please compose yourself before reading the next sentence.

Being positive is not easy.

It's considerably more challenging to be upbeat, happy and positive. And because it's hard work and it takes practice, most people can't be bothered.

'What is to give light must endure burning.'

Viktor Frankl

Our message is, let's get bothered. There's nothing more important that you'll ever do than spread positive, upbeat, energetic, passionate vibes. You'll feel better for it. And, crucially, those around you will respond in a positive manner. We're promising that if you learn to be a 2%er and then do it for the next 30 years it will change your life. You will get markedly different results in terms of relationships, career, happiness – just about everything you do will yield better results when you do it as a positive human being. But there's an even better challenge ahead. A challenge so exciting that it makes my skin tingle (or is

'The difference between "try" and "triumph" is just a little "umph".'

Unknown

that just my dermatitis again?). The real question is, over the next 30 years, how many people can we take with us? How many people can we influence in a positive way? How many can we inspire? Boy, that sounds like worthwhile work.

Let's go back to those who inhabit the rarefied atmosphere of the upper 2%. They're only human so they experience downtime, but their natural habitat is close to the upper reaches of how fab they can feel. They have energy, positivity, radiance and often wear a smile. They're great to have around because they light up the room. So, that leaves us with the original question: Who the hell are these weirdoes – I mean 'positive people'? What do they do that makes them so happy? And what can we learn from them that we can actually put into practice in our own lives?

> 'Why be "ordinary", when you can choose to be "extra-ordinary"? Why live life in black and white when it can be colour?'
>
> *Richard Wilkins*

It makes me smile when delegates on courses come up to me at break time and nod sagely. 'This is just about "positive thinking" isn't it? It's just glass half full stuff.' Absolutely not. In fact, in some quarters, 'positive thinking' is seen as cloud cuckoo land. Barbara Ehrenreich's fab book *Smile or Die* (2010) neatly argues that the current financial crisis has been caused by positive thinking. And it's easy to agree. Banks were lending money willy nilly, not bothering to check if people could actually afford to pay it back. And we were borrowing it! Property prices have always risen, so let's be positive and assume they will forever. *Whoops!*

> 'You can put your boots in the oven but that don't make them biscuits.'
>
> *Dallas DJ, 103.3FM*

And, on a more local level, here's another example of positive thinking gone mad. I cringed when I observed a session in a school where the trainer whipped the teenagers into a frenzy of thinking they could be whatever they wanted. They all whooped with joy as they stated their ambition. We had dozens of astronauts, professional footballers and brain surgeons. And this was Doncaster (sorry Donny, cheap gag!).

There's nothing wrong with ambition and dreaming big. In fact, we actively encourage it (see the later chapter 15 on HUGGs). But *The Art of Being Brilliant* isn't really about positive thinking. It's much more subtle than that. The brilliant Zig Ziglar (2009) sums it up well in the following passage.

Just what can positive thinking do?
To be candid, some people have given positive thinking a bad name. I can't stand to hear some gung-ho individual say that with positive thinking you can just do 'anything'. If you think about that one for a moment, you recognise the absurdity of it. As a ridiculous example, I'm a positive thinker, but I could never slam-dunk a basketball or perform major surgery – or even minor surgery – on anyone and expect that person to survive. Nate Newton, the 300-plus pound lineman for the Dallas Cowboys, is positive, optimistic and outgoing but he'd be a complete failure as a jockey or a ballet dancer.

It's safe to say that positive thinking won't let you do 'anything'. However, it is even safer to say that positive thinking will let you do 'everything' better than negative thinking will. Positive thinking will let you use the ability which you have, and that is awesome. It works this way. You can walk into a dark room, flip on the switch and immediately the room is lighted. Flipping the switch did not generate the electricity; it released the electricity which had been stored. Positive thinking works that way – it releases the abilities which you have.'

Now that's something with which we can concur!

Our final thought in this chapter goes to a great quote that seems to sum up a lot of thinking about young people nowadays:

'The world is passing through troubled times. The young people of today think of nothing but themselves. They have no respect for parents or older people. They are impatient. They talk as if they know everything, and what passes for wisdom with us is foolishness with them. As for the girls, they are forward, immodest and unladylike in speech, behaviour and dress.'

Hard to disagree? Except that this quote is from a sermon preached by Peter the Hermit in AD 1274! Seems that young people have always been frowned upon by the older generation. Maybe it's not the younger generation that needs to change. Maybe it's up to us to chill out a bit.

Check out the questions below:

1. What would you do if the world was going to end one week from today?

2. Jump ahead to the end of your working life. Reflect back on your career. What are the three most important lessons you've learned and why are they so critical?

3. Think of someone who inspires you. What exactly do they do that makes you feel so brilliant?

4. Who are you at your best?

5. It's your 100th birthday and there's a big family party in your honour. Someone is going to stand up and say a few words about you. What would you like them to say?

_____

_____

_____

6. List 10 things you really appreciate but that you take for granted. [7]

_____

_____

_____

_____

_____

_____

_____

_____

_____

7. What are the most important things to have emerged from answering these questions?

_____

_____

_____

[7] We ran this exercise in a workshop once and someone put 'tinned salmon' at the top of his list. Just above his wife and kids!

'I try to take one day at a time but sometimes several days attack me at once.'

Ashleigh Brilliant ©

Chapter 4
GLOWING ON THE OUTSIDE

In which we go retro! Dad gets a brand new Austin Maxi, we discover the truth behind Ready Brek and the 'A Team' gets a mention. We discover why being a Mii could upset you and we experience a life-changing car journey.

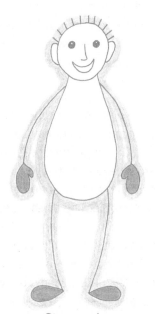

Strange glow...
Is it happiness or does he
live near a nuclear power plant?

There's a term we came across recently – 'entropy'. I don't get a kick out of academia, but I do love language, so I checked it out. Great word! Basically, it's a law of physics that was originally about machines. In simple terms it states that any machine, if left alone, will lose energy. It just seeps away! Therefore new energy has to be applied. Entropy is this 'new energy.'

Let's give you an example from 1974. My dad used to have an old Vauxhall Viva. He bought a new car (a green Austin Maxi with a vinyl roof…nice move Pa!) and never sold the Viva. Every year it sat on the drive, rusting, losing its lustre. It started out red and gradually turned pinky orange. The tyres went flat. It even developed a dent in its bumper, all of its own accord (looking back, I think it was self-harming. Maybe even a cry for help). My dad's Viva was the principle of entropy in action. It wasn't going anywhere. Its energy just seeped away. It became more and more knackered. In the end the scrap man gave my dad a fiver and away it went.

Bear with me…because entropy also applies to people. There's even something called 'corporate entropy.' Literally, organisations and teams can run out of energy. Imagine energy levels on a scale of 0 to 10 where zero is dead and 10 is you on a crazed-up, manic energy explosion. A lot of people seem to be at the 2, 3 or 4 end of the spectrum. Symptoms include a heavy heart on Monday, lethargy, counting down to the weekend and using your evenings to recover from work. What if we could raise you to the 7, 8, 9 end of the spectrum? There's a series of technical terms we use for this like 'alive', 'energetic', 'upbeat' and 'positive'. The symptoms include happiness, creativity, vivacity, a strange glow on the outside and a willingness to take opportunities. You are likely to smile more. Bizarrely, you will also invigorate the people around you.

> 'I don't feel old. I don't feel anything till noon. That's when it's time for my nap.'
>
> *Bob Hope*

There is, of course, a fine line between this ideal state and a 10 – buzzing around like a blue-arsed fly – upsetting people with your positivity. There's a Britishness thing going on here. If we're honest, people who are just too happy get on your wick. If you wake up one morning to find your house has burned down, your partner has left you and the dog is dead, the last thing you need is someone saying 'Every cloud…one door closes…plenty more fish in the sea…'

We certainly don't want to come across all American in our evangelism for personal development. I recently read an American version of some of the material we're going to introduce you to. I won't tell you the author, but he's a very well-known expert in the field. 'I don't have an alarm clock,' he proclaims, 'I have an opportunity clock!' And I felt nauseous. Not in Britain, mate. There's just no way that your average Brit is going to be convinced that her 6 a.m. alarm is an opportunity to leap out of bed and attack life with gusto. This isn't California. The mornings are dark half the year and the weather's often

> 'There was no screaming, no shouting, no clenching of fists or wild exhortation. He simply walked in, picked up the ball, and said, "Let's go."'
>
> *Alf Ramsey about Bobby Moore before world cup 1966*

miserable. And the commute to work is hardly hassle free! We are certainly not advocating happiness and positivity always and forever… just a bit more often.

The good news is that we are all allowed downtime. We don't want you off the happiness scale, grinning inanely at people and rejoicing at the demise of the western European economies. Just up a notch or two (or maybe even three or four). Our point is startlingly simple. If you can increase your energy, you'll be more effective in this crazy millennium. (My dad's Viva represents some of the people we've met over the years!)

Check out the following list. These are the indicators of 'corporate entropy' – sure signs that business energy is slipping away:

1. There is no longer time for celebration.
2. Problem makers outnumber problem solvers.
3. Teams 'over-communicate' and 'under-converse'. (You email the person sitting next to you)
4. The pressures of day-to-day operations push aside our concern for vision and creativity.
5. Too many people have that 'here we go again' feeling.
6. People speak of customers as impositions on their time rather than opportunities to serve.
7. The focus is on surviving the week.
8. The emphasis is on systems rather than people.

So, entropy leads us to a couple of lines of enquiry. Firstly, where does the energy go? And, even more importantly, how can we create more of it? Remember the Ready Brek advert from the

1980s? 'Central Heating for Kids' was the strap line. To refresh your memory, a young fellow scrapes the last bits of Ready Brek from his bowl and develops a rather strange glow on the outside. He then dons hat and coat to go and play with his buddies in the snow. They've not had their Ready Brek and are devoid of the glow. Our chap stands out a mile. He's happier, more positive and warmer than the rest. You can see the difference! On the energy scale, they are a 3 and he's a 9.[8]

So, this begs the question, how do we do it? How do we retain a glow on the outside when the world is so damned negative? And your work colleagues are stuck in doom mode. And the weather's rubbish. And it's all repeats, game shows, cooking programmes or reality nonsense on the telly. And the *Daily Mail* tells us hoodies are everywhere (and they've all got knives). And work pressures are massive. Interest rates are up and it's bad for borrowers. And the rate goes down so the media screams that it's bad for savers.

> 'I have a new philosophy. I'm only going to dread one day at a time.'
>
> *Charles M. Schultz*

I suffered the ultimate insult last week – we bought a game called 'Wii Fit'. Plugged it in. Stood on it and the damned thing deemed me overweight. It made my Mii character short and fat! Being insulted by a stranger is bad enough, but by my TV! Doh!

It seems society is deliberately forcing us into a negative state. It's like being cornered by a pack of rabid dogs.

---

[8] *The Ready Brek advert was taken off the telly in 1986, shortly after the Chernobyl disaster. They deemed that the glow on the outside wasn't seen to be such a healthy image!*

So, where's the good news? And the success stories? The sunshine? And the non-hoody teenagers?

Shall we let you into a secret?

It's all out there, we just don't focus on it.

The media likes to keep it a secret and we've become conditioned to look at the negative side of things. And, as we'll see in a later chapter, you get what you focus on! The result is that we sometimes manage to fight off the rabid dogs of doom and achieve 'brilliance' in spurts. We can all feel great sometimes (we call these times 'Saturdays'). But, hark, I hear barking. The frothy mouthed beasts are back. 'Brilliance' seems impossible to sustain.

'Nothing travels faster than the speed of light with the possible exception of bad news, which obeys its own special laws.'

Douglas Adams, *Mostly Harmless* (1992)

Before we start in earnest, let's think back to your early years. You see, when we are born, when we enter this world for the first time, we arrive perfect.

When Andy W was little, he remembers running round like a crazy fool, in to everything. (Hm, thinking about it, not much has changed.) If his Ma didn't keep a close eye on him, he was off, exploring, curious about his surroundings. He was constantly excited, wanting to do new things, meet new friends, play, laugh and make the most of life. He was curious. He didn't think about what he was doing – he just did it. Andy recalls one of his earliest memories – watching the Lombard car rally on television – and that was it, he was going to be a famous rally driver, the best in the world. There was no question of whether it was possible, he had decided it was meant to be.

'The average child laughs about 400 times per day, the average adult laughs only 15 times per day. What happened to the other 385 laughs?'

Anonymous

That is, of course, until he saw the A-team for the first time and decided he was going to get some friends together and drive around in a black van helping those in need, protecting the innocent from bad guys. Andy remembers his mum telling him they were going to Spain on holiday. 'I ain't gettin' on no plane,' was his razor sharp reply. 'Yes siree,' he beams, "on the run for a crime I didn't commit,"' that was the life for me.[9]

As adults we have possibly lost touch with one of the greatest gifts we have – the gift of curiosity. Have you noticed that children can get really curious about anything new? They can watch a beetle crawling on the ground for what seems like an age, totally involved in what they're doing, observing its every movement, wondering what will happen next. And then they flip it over onto its back and watch it kick its legs in the air as another significant chunk of time passes.

I used to love Christmas. I would start getting excited and curious about what Santa would be bringing me, probably around August time. My dad would always tell me I would be getting

---

[9] *Andy's A-Team dream nearly came true – except he's on the run for a crime he did commit.*

coal and an orange or, if I was lucky, a piece of wood and a pen knife so I could whittle myself a canoe. It didn't really matter what I opened on Christmas Day – it was always a feeling of excitement and curiosity.

Here's an interesting thought for you. When was the last time you couldn't sleep for excitement? Or the last time you stopped to smell some flowers? Or the last time you got up especially early to take a walk at sunrise? Or the last time you deliberately splashed in a puddle?

We know that children have amazing imaginations. Why does it get duller as we get older? Why do the majority of people stop dreaming and lose touch with their child-like ability? Maybe it gets hammered out of us. Or we get knocked back. Or we read the *Daily Mail* and are indoctrinated into the belief that the end of the world is nigh. We now have BBC News 24, so we can have bad news piped to us around the clock! Or the reality of mortgage, career and kids means we haven't got time to dream.

> 'I spent a lot of money on booze, birds and fast cars. The rest I just squandered.'
>
> *George Best*

One possible contributing factor is the massive unconscious influence our parents have over us as we are growing up. And teachers are constantly drilling in to us to work hard, get a good job and to stop living in a fairy tale world, repeating the message in one form or another that 'life isn't easy'. They've probably got a point; I'm sure life isn't meant to be fun all the time.

That leads us to a few questions:

1. Well, what is life supposed to be then?

2. Why are we here?

3. What's the point in having a great imagination?

4. What is the secret to life?

5. How do I make sure I don't waste it?

6. What is 'success'?

7. Why does sour cream have a sell-by date?

8. If toast always lands butter-side down, and cats always land on their feet, what happens if you strap toast onto the back of a cat and drop it?

Andy and I ponder these kinds of questions. In fact, people have often called us a right pair of ponderers (or something similar, at least).

The point we're making is that, as children, we do listen and are constantly taking in what people, especially adults, are telling us. We are like sponges.[10] We tend to copy what they do. We learn our thinking and behaviours from those closest to us. Learning comes naturally. Andy W has a little girl, Olivia, who is nine years old. In Andy's words, 'The light of my life. The joy in my heart. The inspiration in my soul. And, more often than not, the pain in my behind.' I always remember a conversation we had, it took place when she was no older than four. Travelling back from my parents in Morecambe, on the M1 just north of Sheffield (that's a nice run in the car, you should do it one Sunday!). It went like this:

Olivia: 'Father Darling.' (She is very well spoken for someone born in Mansfield.)

Andy: 'What?' (I'm not very well spoken for someone born in Morecambe.) I replied, whilst noticing her in the rear view mirror looking out of the back window towards the sky.

Olivia: 'Did God create the sky Daddy?' she asked with a real look of curiosity on her face.

Andy: 'Yes, God created the sky' (nodding wisely, but not entirely convinced, trying to reconcile the whole 'Old Testament' with the 'Big Bang' conundrum).

Olivia: 'Can I create the sky, Daddy?' she replied as quick as a flash.

Andy: (chuckling knowingly) 'Probably not, sweetheart.'

---

[10] *Interesting thought: if you removed all the world's sponges from the ocean, would the sea level rise?*

Olivia: 'Did God create the birds, Daddy?' she asked, still looking out of the window.

Andy: 'Yes, darling. God probably did create the birds.'

Olivia: 'Can I create the birds?'

Andy: 'Probably not.'

We went back and forth – mountains, oceans, grass – she would ask me whether God created them and I had to inform her that yes, He did, and that she couldn't. All the time she was looking more and more confused about the fact that God could create all these wonderful things and she couldn't. I was thinking where the heck has this conversation come from and, probably more importantly, where was it heading?

Olivia paused for a minute and I breathed a sigh of relief. Maybe she'll change the subject, I hoped. It was then that she posed the killer question…

Olivia: 'Why Daddy? Why can God create those things and I can't?'

I thought long and hard as I didn't want to give her a standard adult reply such as 'just…because' or, even worse, 'go and ask your mum'. I came up with something that I'm proud of to this very day.

Andy: 'Sweetheart, God created all those things so you don't have to. They are already here for you to enjoy, so you can focus on what it is you want to achieve with your life.'

Have that! Quite a heavy answer for a four-year-old, yet I have always thought you should speak to children as real people.

Olivia: 'Can God do a handstand?"

'Insanity is hereditary: You can get it from your children.'

Sam Levinson, American actor, screenwriter and director

Chapter 5
CAN GOD DO
A HANDSTAND?

In which we grapple with Buddhism, learn about the value of not having toothache, are introduced to a fab new toaster and find out stuff they don't tell you at antenatal classes. Two little girls are introduced to the world (one of which might be a Smurf) and we learn all about hereditary thinking.

What?
At my age?

Andy and I need to come clean here. We're not religious in any way, shape or form. I did once read a book on Buddhism which helped me greatly. The advice on page one was to 'wake up every morning and be grateful you've not got toothache'. A bit bizarre when I read it but I actually did that for a few weeks. The alarm goes at 6 am. I poke a toe out from under the duvet and it shoots back undercover. Too early. Too dark. Too cold. I slowly come to consciousness. Another day. Same old routine. But no! My hand strokes my jaw. No toothache. Yippee! What an awesome start to the day and I leap out of bed, energised and up for it. Sounds daft? Try it, it works. And it's not really about toothache. The principle is very profound. Thank God (or your lucky stars, depending on your belief system) we can get out of bed at all. Think about it. When was the last time you thanked your kidneys? Or your heart for pumping all that glorious oxygenated blood? Or your ears or eyes? Wow, we're lucky people! As soon as you start to attach a value to your health you will immediately feel more energetic. Being alive is the best thing ever!

> 'Arthur hoped and prayed that there wasn't an afterlife. Then he realised there was a contradiction there and merely hoped that there wasn't an afterlife.'
>
> Douglas Adams, *Life, the Universe, and Everything* (1982)

Our basic knowledge of religion (Christianity based … and it is basic) is that the Bible says God created the world. But Mr Darwin and his followers say that we evolved from swamp monsters. Either way, both theories are flawed (sorry, that probably upsets just about everyone!). We've reached the point of 'right now' in evolutionary history without an instruction manual.

Bear with me while I tell you about my new toaster. The old toaster went kaput in January. It was a wedding gift so I've got no experience of ever purchasing a toaster. I drove to a soulless, out-of-town shopping centre and purchased a brand spanking new toaster. I got lucky, it was January and there was a sale. Their top of the range toaster (four slices, brushed silver, cruise control, the works) was a mere £15. I nearly bought two, but there's only so much toast that one family can eat. I got the toaster home and unpacked it. She's a beauty, gleaming and aerodynamic, not like the old, green two-slicer that had given up on us. Before I started experimenting with my new, sleek 'Toastomatic 2000', I noticed it came with an instruction booklet. I'm not normally the type of bloke who goes in for instructions. Ikea furniture? Bish, bash, bosh – knock it together. So what if the shelves are wonky and I've got a dozen bits left over and a silly Allen key thing? Mobile phones – same principle. Cast the booklet to one side and get my porky fingers tapping on a few keys. Trial and error. I can usually work it out.

But this time it was different. I clutched the booklet and made for my fave chair. I was feeling warm-hearted, possibly elated by my brushed silver toaster. Somebody had spent time writing this booklet and I was determined to read it. I owed it to them. I turned the pages. Twelve languages! Impressive. I decided to just read the English. Found it. The first four pages were Health and Safety. Apparently toast can be very dangerous. It's basically very hot bread, so be careful out there everybody. And don't stick a fork in the toaster or use the toaster while you're in the bath. Sensible advice, if, I may say, a little over-cautious. Eventually I found the actual instructions on how to make toast. And I'd like to share it with you. Ready? Here goes…

1. Insert bread (or muffin, bagel, etc.)
2. Turn knob to the colour you want it (from snow white to carbon black)
3. Push the lever down (unless you're in the bath, remember?)
4. Wait
5. Toast pops up
6. Remove it, butter it and eat

Twelve languages! Someone's put an awful lot of work into that toaster manual. Hang in there; this will make sense in a minute…

Please rewind to 12 May 1995. I was about to become a dad. Louise was in Derby City Hospital and I was stroking her forehead. Thirty-six hours later I'm still stroking her forehead and still no baby. Various doctors have been in and done examinations (things you wouldn't want another man to ever do to your wife, even if he has got gloves on). No baby. Stuck at three inches dilation. They've given Louise some drugs to help move things on but the baby's not for birthing. Quite suddenly, Louise's ankles swell and within ten minutes she's being wheeled into theatre for a Caesarean. I get all dressed up in green surgeon gear and follow her in. It's an epidural so Louise is dead from the waist down. I resume forehead stroking duty and commentate to my wife as the surgeons go about their work. Five minutes and a small incision later, a very small scrap of a child is pulled from her mum's tummy (have you seen Alien?).

Thankfully, these are professional people. Cords are cut, the slime wiped off the child and it's handed to me. I'm a dad. Six weeks earlier than expected too! Congratulations from all the team. And then they abandon me and my newborn and return to the lady with big ankles. There's poking, prodding and sewing to be done.

There I am left, literally, holding the baby. The as-yet-unnamed child weighs in at a tiny four and a half pounds. It's an emotional moment. Father meets daughter for the very first time. I stare adoringly at my first born. And my first words? The momentous welcome to the world? 'It's got eyes!' I exclaimed as the tot stared up at me. She's wrapped in a white blanket with a tiny baby foot hanging out. 'And feet…with toes!' (I do appreciate that these first words to my newborn could have been more profound. I will make sure my final words are much better.)

The birth of Andy W's daughter is also a superb story. On arrival in the labour room he was handed a cardboard sick bowl and instructed to waft it in front of his wife. 'We hadn't practised this at antenatal classes,' he explains in a deadpan way. 'We'd done breathing and pain relief. Maybe I missed the class on wafting sick bowls?' The first thing he noticed was that his newborn daughter was blue and thought his wife had given birth to a Smurf. 'And my baby was covered in slime!' When asked if he would like to kiss his new arrival, Andy replied, 'You couldn't run a sponge over her first could you please?'

And the point of these autobiographical stories? No manual. The toaster comes with health warnings and instructions in twelve languages when actually it's dead simple. Yet the most complex piece of kit on Earth, a human life, comes with no instruction booklet. We literally make it up as we go along.

So, can I just explore this a tiny bit further?
11 May 1995, I'm not a dad.
12 May 1995, I *am* a dad.

All of a sudden my life has changed. *Dramatically*. It's called 'growing up'. I have a tiny scrap of a human being, with lots of spare skin, who is entirely dependent on me (and Louise, to be fair. You could argue that the boobies thing makes the tot more dependent on Lou than on me).

And as we feed our kids, they grow. And crawl. And explore. And think.

Here's something interesting to ponder: *Who taught you how to think?*

Furrow your brow and rub your chin for a moment while you consider the question. Because, I put it to you that nobody formally taught you how to think. Nobody ever actually sat you down and said, 'OK mate, this is how it's done. This is a thinking lesson.' There's no GCSE in 'positive thinking'.[11] You have to think to get the answers but 'thinking' isn't taught. In fact, we cram our children full of reading, maths, science, cooking, PE, French, geography and media studies, yet the most important piece of kit – their brain – remains a mystery.

_____

[11] *Although apparently there is an AS qualification in 'Critical Thinking', which says it all, really.*

So, if nobody actually taught you to think, where did your thinking come from? Are you ready for the truth about how you learned to think?

You made it up!
You kind of learned it via osmosis.

When you were tiny, your parents and guardians had a way of thinking that they imbued you with. And then you went to school and met 30 other kids in your class and they all had a way of thinking. You wanted to fit in so you did what they did (not knowing that they were making it up as well) and your teachers imparted a way of thinking too (they were also making it up, albeit from a slightly more experienced vantage point). But, the most crucial people in all of this were your parents. So, if you're still with me, let's probe a little deeper. Who taught your parents how to think? That's right – their parents. And who taught your grandparents to think? Brilliant, you've got it. Their parents. And they got it from their parents, etc.

So, what we've ended up with is quite a fixed way of thinking, passed down to us through the generations. Often it's a very defensive way of thinking. It has changed a little but the essence is exactly the same. Our way of thinking is passed down to us.

> 'My father had a profound influence on me, he was a lunatic.'
>
> *Spike Milligan*

Keep an open mind on this next question, because it's a biggy. We've established that nobody actually taught you to think. And think of all the thinking you've done over your lifetime. All the thinking that everyone on the planet's been doing and consider this – what if we've been doing it wrong?

That's nearly as good as 'Can God do a handstand?' What if there was a better way? A way of thinking that freed you from the shackles of negativity that have pervaded generation after generation. A way of thinking that gave you energy. A way of thinking that made you stand out in a crowd. And a set of habits that would change your life. Do you want some good news?

There is!

In the next couple of chapters we have provided a brief instruction manual for your mind. After that, we turn our attention to the science of 'Positive Psychology', revealing the habits of how to stay positive. It's deadly simple and it's mightily good stuff. Read on, your mental software upgrade awaits!

Your amazing life (so far)...

Spend a few minutes thinking about your life to date – what has had a significant impact on you so far?

1. List milestones and events that have been important.

_____

_____

_____

_____

_____

_____

_____

2. Who has been instrumental in shaping your thinking?

3. What achievements are you pleased about?

4. What 'less than happy' experiences have influenced you?

5. Write a list of things you feel good about in your life.

6. Reflect on why you do the job you do. What's the best thing about your job? (You're not allowed to say 'going home'.)

7. What is, for you, 'success'?

8. Interviews with the elderly do not report that people regret the things they have done, but rather, people talk about the things they regret not having done. What are your thoughts on this?

9. What are the most important things life has taught you?

10. List 20 things you want to do before you die.

'There cannot be a stressful crisis next week. My schedule is already full.'

Henry Kissinger

Chapter 6
BUSYNESS AS USUAL

In which we examine life as a blue-arsed fly, look at how your brain works and why most people get stuck in a cycle of sameness. We continue the retro theme with some Freddy Kruger before introducing Heather and Mick's big night out. We finish with the answer to the age-old question, 'Why are all men bastards?'

Bob was so busy that he had developed a blue arse

'Busyness' is a term that's made it into the English language. In fact, it's not just sneaked in quietly, it's shoulder-barged in as a way of life. Busyness is an epidemic that's swept the nation. I remember sitting in Economics 'A' level in the late 1980s and learning that by the year 2000 we'd all have loads of spare time. Robots would be doing the work and people would be enjoying days of leisure. We'd be in the gym or on ocean cruises. We'd have pots of money and loads of time. It was billed as future bliss. Well, it's clear we were sold a pup. Leisure time? It's like the mythical thing they call a 'lunch hour'! Most people are working longer hours not shorter ones. And life's got faster not slower.

If you're as old as me you'll remember 'memos'. These were hand written notes that you placed in a wire tray. At the end of the day the magic admin fairy would deliver them around the organisation. Five or six days later you'd get a reply. Five or six days! Now we've got text messaging and emails. You email the person who's sitting next to you and copy every man and his dog in to cover your back. Organisations over-communicate and under-converse. Knowledge is at our fingertips. Google has opened up a world of instant information. Then there's fast food and microwave meals… ping… 'tea's ready'. My wife made a Christmas list and inked in at number one was a 'ten second kettle'. You don't have to wait for a cuppa nowadays. The kettle boils instantly! (I think she's missing the point that the whole raison d'être of a cup of tea is that you sit down for a couple of minutes while the kettle boils.) Last night, I watched the BBC One-minute World News. A 100mph summary, crammed into 60 seconds, because we haven't got time for proper news. You may have heard of a phenomenon called 'speed dating'. Think about it. You've got 45 seconds to decide if you want to spend the rest of your life with this person.[12] Why? 'Busyness', that's why! Because you haven't got time to devote to nurturing a proper relationship. Many people spend more time searching for a house than they do for a partner!

And before I rest my case on the 'busyness epidemic' I'm ashamed to say that I recently contributed a children's story for an anthology of 'One Minute Bedtime Stories' for busy parents who don't have time to read a whole chapter. I know. And I'm ashamed of myself for doing it. Even worse, when I knew the book was coming out my initial reaction was 'great idea' because now I can get the bedtime story over with quickly. In our house it had become a bit of a chore – I was always busy doing emails or writing or preparing for the next day's course and Ollie would always want his dad to read a bedtime story. So I'd sit on the end of my son's bed and go through the motions. I'd read quickly so I could get back to my emails. You could test me on the chapter and I would have no idea of what I'd just read. Sometimes I'd even skip a couple of pages in my race to get to the end. The trouble is that Ollie's a bright lad and he knew when I was missing bits out. So he'd tell me. And I'd deny it. And we'd end up arguing because he wanted the proper version and I wanted the quick version! So the bedtime story was an annoyance! A frustration. A hindrance to my evening.

The solution – I've learned to change my thinking. The old me treated the bedtime story as a 'to do' on my list. Something that had to be ticked in the race to get through the day. A chore. Nowadays? I view reading a bedtime story as a reward at the end

---

[12] Here's a new word if you're a younger reader. 'Courting'. This is what we did in the olden days, before the interweb. 'Courting' would take about 11 years. It was the very slow process of meeting someone, getting to know them and then – get this – you'd get married and then move in together. In that order! There's an audible gasp if I explain this to teenagers. 'OMG!'

of my day. I ask myself a very simple question, 'How would the best dad in the world read this story?' I don't judge 'success' on how quickly I can get back downstairs, but on how engaged we can get in the story. A small change in my thinking has resulted in a huge improvement in the bedtime ritual. It's bliss!

'There is a theory which states that if ever anyone discovers exactly what the Universe is for and why it is here, it will instantly disappear and be replaced by something even more bizarre and inexplicable. There is another theory which states that this has already happened.'

Douglas Adams, *The Restaurant at the End of the Universe (1982)*

At a basic biological level, human beings are filters. That's all we do – take information in and process it. We have an innate desire to make sense of the world. So, we let the information we want get through and discard the rest. At any moment in time we are being bombarded by two million stimuli. If you're lucky, you've got five senses that enable you to absorb information: sight, smell, taste, touch and hearing.

If we were to actually process every piece of data that hits our senses we would become overloaded. We'd all end up locked in white padded rooms drooling on each other. In our research we've come across a lot of contradictory studies in the area of information processing. But the basic point is this – there are millions of stimuli vying for our conscious awareness. Our nervous system processes only a tiny proportion of that information. Basically, the vast majority of what's happening around us is filtered out.

Imagine someone tipping a lorry load of two million straws onto you and trying to catch them all. It would be impossible. Our nervous system works on the same principle. So, to protect us from going crazy, the information passes through three in-built filters. These are:

1. Deletion
2. Distortion
3. Generalisation

1. *Deletion*
A deletion is where our nervous system just ignores any information which it thinks is not relevant. Read the following phrase:

Paris in the
the Spring

Now go back and take a closer look at the phrase. If you haven't already noticed, it has the word 'the' in it twice. However, in order to make sense of the text our brain automatically deletes one of the words. Your brain is doing this on your behalf all the time.

Let's try another. Obviously, it's harder to catch you out second time round. Maybe you want to try this out on someone else.

How many 'F's are in the following sentence?

FINISHED FILES ARE THE RESULT OF YEARS OF
SCIENTIFIC STUDY COMBINED WITH THE EXPERIENCE
OF MANY YEARS OF EXPERTS [13]

'Deletion' takes away much of the superfluous information that bombards our senses. However, and this is the profound bit, many people are deleting the wrong information.

Let me give you an example. I'm queuing at Morrisons, in Bolton on 22 December. It's a stunning day, with beautiful blue skies outside. Short sleeves weather. More May than December. For as long as I live I will not get a better December day in the UK. The checkout lady finds time to chat to the lady who's in front of me. While she's beeping her cat food through she says, in a passing-the-day-kind-of-way, 'Isn't it a lovely day?'

And the customer looks slightly un-nerved and replies, 'Is it love? I only ever see the rain.'

Well, I nearly dropped my Newcastle Brown in horror. The poor woman. 'I only ever see the rain!' She's deleting the good weather! Focusing on the negative to the point that her mind never consciously recognises a good day but is, instead, tuned into the bad. It's not just the bad weather she's tuned into. Traffic jams, for sure. And, to her, all teenagers will be 'hoodies' and everyone on the dole a sponger and all 149 TV channels are rubbish.

One more quick example. I ran a course last week which went

---

[13] *Most people count three or four 'F's. There are in fact six!*

really well. Of the 40 delegates, 39 rated the course as 'excellent'. There was one who put 'good'. And I cursed and swore all the way home, focusing on the 'good', my mind deleting the 39 'excellents'.

2. *Distortion*

The second filter we use, which enables us to make sense of our environment, is distortion. Distortions are when we adjust the data to fit our view of the world. You hear half a story and your mind automatically fills in the gaps to make sense of it. We spend time in the Tesco queue making up all sorts of assumptions about people according to the contents of their trolley. Our mind has a fraction of the story so we literally make up the rest. 'Lasagne for one! And a box of Maltesers. Comfort eating. Oh deary me. Poor singleton.' The reality could be that the lady's husband has gone out with his mates, and she's really looking forward to a quiet night in with a DVD and a ready meal followed by a box of Maltesers. So, actually, she's toe-curlingly happy.

Try this general knowledge question for size: 'How many animals of each species did Moses take onto the Ark?'

A fairly simple question? Most people instinctively know the answer because they distort the sentence to give it the meaning they want. And they come up with 'two'. But that means most people get it wrong! The answer is 'none'. Moses didn't take any animals onto the Ark because he was parting the Red Sea at the time. It was his pal Noah that led them in two by two.

Radek Ossowski's picture below is a favourite of ours. He calls it 'The Tree of Life'. Have a closer look and see if you can spot the illusion.

Image used with permission of Radek Ossowski

(Psst. The picture also shows a baby.)

In a similar vein, advertising company Lowe/SSP3 created a series of clever images to promote the Colsubsidio Book Exchange. They used the slogan 'Come with a Story and Leave with Another.' Can you recognise the books being referenced below?[14]

Image used with permission of Lowe/SSP3

---

[14] *Snow White and Sherlock Holmes*

Why are we showing you these weird images? Because you can interpret them in more than one way. Have you ever come out of the cinema and discussed the film you've just seen? You were blown away by the special effects and exciting storyline, totally invigorated and on the edge of your seat. And your partner had snoozed through the whole thing!

Your nervous system distorts information according to what you are focusing on at the time. Imagine you are in, alone, late at night. It's dark and rainy outside, you can hear the wind howling through the trees and the rain is pounding against your windows. You are watching *A Nightmare on Elm Street* and Freddy is just about to slice someone in two with his big, blood soaked, razor sharp fingers. Then you hear it outside, slow footsteps dragging their way onto your porch. Now, I ask you, whose footsteps, right at that moment, are you going to hear? Before you know it, you're behind the sofa!

However, in the same situation, you are watching a Walt Disney film. Whom are you going to imagine the footsteps belong to now? The point being, you will imagine two completely different scenarios because you are distorting the external information coming into your nervous system in conjunction with what you are focusing on at the time.

I'm sure you have experienced saying something to someone and they get the wrong end of the stick, or have given someone an instruction and they go off and do the complete opposite of what you said. Andy W recalls telling his ex-wife 'I love you'. 'I thought it meant spending time together and cuddling whilst we carved out our future. But she distorted it to mean I should spend my time mowing the lawn, putting shelves up and spending my weekends in B&Q.'

3. Generalisation

Our third and final filter, which allows us to make sense of the external information, is generalisation. Generalisations aid us in learning. Once we have learned or experienced something we tend to generalise that that's how it is. Generalisation is incredibly useful as we don't have to re-learn activities all the time. If we didn't generalise, everything would be new to us all the time. For example, if we didn't generalise that cars were driven the same way, every time we got into a different car we would have to learn to drive all over again. If you have ever driven a car and the indicators and windscreen wipers were on different control stalks, it takes a while to get used to. You want to indicate or you are turning a corner and your windscreen gets another cleaning – until that generalisation is broken. (You then get back into your own car and have to reverse the generalisation again!)

To prove how we generalise, an experiment was carried out. One hundred students were asked to take part. They were simply told that all they had to do was open a door. The information they were given was that the door would definitely open. Sounds simple, right? However, the door was set up with the hinges on the same side as the door handle, meaning the door would only swing open when pushed at the opposite side to the door handle. Despite the fact that it still doesn't appear to be that difficult, the results were quite astonishing. Out of the 100

Dean wasn't looking forward to the test

people asked to take part not one of them managed to break the generalisation of how a door opened!

Let's take the principle further. People may have one bad experience in life (usually when they are a small child) and that's it, they then generalise that all experiences which are similar will be bad.[15]

And here's another example. Have you ever heard a woman saying 'All men are b*****ds'? In reality they have probably had one bad experience (OK, maybe a couple) and bang, that's it,

---

[15] *Fact: baby monkeys learn to be afraid of poisonous snakes by watching the reaction of older monkeys.*

the entire male gender is rendered of questionable parentage. Incidentally, some women then go around with that belief – and guess what kind of men they attract.

Generalisations like the ones above are there to simplify life. How many times have you heard things like:

'Teenagers nowadays – they're all hoodies.' *(What, every single one of them?)*

'We go abroad because it's always miserable in August.' *(Every day? Every August? Amazing.)*

'Nobody ever listens to me.' *(What, nobody? Ever?)*

'All politicians are corrupt.' *(OK, got me there. Some generalisations are spot on. Only joking, of course!)*

Generalisations also serve to protect us. We experience something that we view as unfavourable and we build walls (metaphorical ones in our minds, not real ones that brickies build) that protect us from the bad stuff happening again. For example, we don't dare love anyone ever again because someone broke our heart twenty years ago.

The problem with these metaphorical protective walls, though, is that they also limit us – they stop us living to our maximum enjoyment.

So, our brain automatically deletes, distorts and generalises the world around us so we can make sense of it. These are our filters. Think of it like panning for gold. The only problem is that some people are accidentally filtering out the nuggets and collecting the gravel!

Our advice is to be consciously aware of when you're deleting, distorting and generalising. You can't stop doing it but an awareness gives you a better chance of panning for gold rather than gravel. Search out new experiences and new ways of viewing the world.

Check these out for starters:

1. Go on a favourite walk and try to look out for at least ten things you have never noticed before. Trust me there will be hundreds. Take pleasure in noticing them.

2. Look around the room you're in. Now look at it again and this time notice the blue items.

3. Agree with a point of view that you wouldn't normally agree with. Check out the world from this perspective. Marvel at it. Be fascinated. Find some pleasure in it.

4. Watch a TV programme you wouldn't normally watch or listen to a radio station you wouldn't normally listen to. Decide to enjoy it.

5. Ask your kids if you can listen to one of their CDs and be delighted with what you hear. Tell them how wonderful their taste in music is. (Ok, this may be a step too far!)

And, finally, in this chapter we want to indulge you with our absolute favourite bit of deletion, distortion and generalisation. I'm sure you're aware that some people are left brain dominant while others have a more pronounced right brain. And that males and females think differently. And that we interpret events in different ways. Everyone must also be familiar with the notion that men can only do one thing at once.[16]

---

[16] This is, of course, a generalisation in its own right. But it goes some way to explain that when we're reading the newspaper, we cannot hear you!

Check out the following piece. Our work brings us into plenty of one-on-one coaching situations and we've changed the names here for obvious reasons. The couple in question have tried marriage counselling and turned to us for guidance. After 15 years of marriage, they've begun to drift apart. We talked to 'Heather' and 'Mick' about their feelings. In fact, to give you some context, this was a very sensitive time because these interviews took place shortly after 'Mick' moved out...

Heather's story

'Mick was in a strange mood when we met in the pub tonight. He was a lot quieter than normal. A bit distant really. It's been really difficult without him and I guess I was hoping he'd be really pleased to see me. We had a quick drink, with lots of silences. I suggested we take a taxi back to his flat – maybe he'd open up to me a bit if I got him out of the pub? As we drove back I told him I still loved him. And do you know what his reply was? Nothing! He put his arm around me and stared out of the window. What's that supposed to mean? He never tells me he loves me. Even when we were together he only ever said it twice. Anyway, when we got back to his place we cuddled up on the sofa and watched some trashy Saturday night TV. I tried to get the conversation going but all I got were some grunts. Typical! I'd forgotten how uncommunicative he can be. I can't help loving him though. I mean, we were together for 15 years. We're still married for heaven's sake. So when he kissed me I couldn't resist. We ended up having sex and guess what? He fell asleep! I'm convinced the relationship is over. I mean, he'd rather sleep when we've got so much to talk about. In the end, I just cried myself to sleep.'

Mick's story

'Met Heather for a beer. Was knackered. United lost. Got a shag, though.'

'It's hard to speak of our need for awe when everything, even a new kind of biscuit, is routinely described as "awesome".'

Alain De Botton

Chapter 7
PANTS ON THE OUTSIDE

In which we look at why most people are like Popeye but without the spinach. We examine belief systems, get some new wheels, experience daylight robbery and squeeze in the word 'temerity' which, in our opinion, isn't used enough.

Smithers got the idea from a problem solving course

You've probably seen the *Superman* movie, with Christopher Reeve. I'm old enough to remember the hype when it came out. 'You'll believe a man can fly,' they convinced us. Pah! The effects were actually laughable and the movie no great shakes, but there are elements that I love. For example, when Lois Lane is standing on her balcony, 45 stories up, looking out over the city lights. It's a balmy evening. Superman flies down and lands on her balcony. She looks stunned, and for good reason. After all, this is a guy in a Lycra suit, wearing his pants on the outside. With a silly strand of hair tweaked to look all boyish. Oh, and he can fly! (Told you it was barmy!)

Lois is a reporter and can't let go of her journalistic instincts. So she asks him, 'What do you stand for, Superman?'

And he puffs out his chest with pride before announcing cheesily, 'Truth, Justice and the American way!'

As sickly and hammy as that may be, I rather like it. Because, at least he knew! At least he could quote a set of values and beliefs. We don't need to have the same beliefs and values as Superman. We certainly don't need to wear our pants on the outside. But knowing what our values are is a fine starting point.

Let's defer to Richard Wilkins, the UK's self-styled 'Minister of Inspiration'. Richard's favourite saying is that 'we're all superheroes, pretending to be normal people'. Most of the people I know are hiding it well. It's as though they've got Kryptonite in their socks! Or, to put it another way, I know a lot of Popeyes who hate spinach!

Jenny was special.
She had counted to infinity. Twice.

When I was growing up we had proper superheroes. They had an outfit, or a power, or they went green and muscley. In short, they were special.

When my son was little he used to watch Bob the Builder DVDs and, for a long time, I didn't get it. I would shake my head. What's the point of Bob? He's not a superhero. There's no special outfit and it's not as if he's had an accident with a Black & Decker that's turned him into the 'contractor of choice'. He's just a builder!

Until one day I sat down and watched an episode of Bob. Wow![17] Bob never ever turns up at a job with his bum crack hanging out of his jeans, sucking in his breath in that 'bringer of bad tidings' kind of way. 'Oh heck! Who put those skirting boards in, love? And that plumbing? Best put the kettle on before we start. Three sugars. It's gonna be a big job.'

Quite the opposite. Bob turns up with a smile and a wave. And he doesn't turn up on his own. He brings his team…Scoop, Muck,

---

[17] *Treat yourself to the box set, series 1.*

Dizzy, Wendy, Roly and Spud. And they sing and dance their way through every episode. And when the going gets tough, Bob doesn't jack it in and grumble off to the pub. Bob remains cheerful in a crisis and he shouts to his team, 'Can we fix it?'

And, here's the best bit – his team shouts back, 'Yes we can!'

Now that's the kind of builder I want to employ. A 'can-do' guy with an empowered team. I appreciate that I might be looking too academically at Bob, but it seems to me that Bob has the same skills and tools as all the other builders. What differentiates him is his extraordinary attitude. In fact it's his attitude that marks Bob out as being the best builder in the world!

So, maybe it's not a case of having to wear your pants on the outside. Maybe we can achieve superhero status by being the best version of ourselves that we can possibly muster at any moment in time. And maybe that's connected to our values.

Complete the next few sentences. There's no right or wrong. The aim is to begin to unearth your core beliefs and values:

People are...

Happiness is...

Love means...

Money is...

Work is...

Family is...

Success is...

We naturally assume people have the same values as us. This is the reason that you can't understand some people's actions.

Which leads me onto a story that falls into the 'painful but true' category. I'll keep it brief. I had two chores, to do a big shop at Tesco and a change of tyres at Kwikfit. I combined them, dropping my car off at the garage and walking ten minutes to

Tesco while the work was underway. Multi-tasking! It was winter. It was snowing and I felt great. I filled my trolley and left the shop. I hadn't quite thought my plan through because now I had a trolley full of goodies and no car! It was going to be too awkward to trundle the trolley to the garage so I left it for ten minutes while I jogged down the road to pick up my re-tyred motor. I figured that the snow would help keep my frozen stuff frozen. And what a fine job the Kwikfit boys had done. I drove back to Tesco to reclaim my trolley (you've guessed, haven't you) and drove round the car park looking for it. I parked up and began a search by foot. The trolley was gone so I went inside and asked. In my mind, obviously, a good Samaritan had trundled it inside for safe-keeping.

I won't bore you with the anguish and consequent gnashing of teeth. Suffice to say the trolley, and my weekly shopping, had done a bunk. Someone had had the temerity and nerve to see a trolley that had been left for ten minutes – and stolen it. The thieving b******s! I've only told that story once. Obviously, everybody laughed (at me, not with me I might add). 'How could you be so stupid?' someone asked.

But to me, I wasn't being stupid. Honesty is a core value. And because I'm honest, I naturally assume everyone else is.[18] That event shook my belief system and I have to admit to eyeing people suspiciously for a while afterwards.

Last year I went to the cashpoint and someone had left their wad of notes. There they were, a bevy of virgin twenties, neat and crisp and even. There was nobody around to claim the dosh so what's a person supposed to do? I took the notes and pocketed them.

[18] If the thief is reading this it's not too late to redeem yourself. Help yourself to the turkey. But can I have my Speckled Hen back?

And then I took the cash into the bank and handed it in.

There are no 'right' or 'wrong' values, just different values (although I'm really struggling to justify 'dishonesty' as a valid value). Your values will be driving your behaviour and the results you are achieving in your life. Values are like an anchor. They give you a grounding. Think of a boat analogy. The boat can drift a little but the anchor drags it back.

> 'Eagles may soar high, but weasels don't get sucked into jet engines.'
>
> *Attributed to both Jason Hutchison and John Benfield*

Customer service is our top priority.
Now, next agenda item, our new call centre in Outer Mongolia

More and more companies these days are coming up with 'company values'. Often, the board of executives have a big meeting and come up with values that they want the business to adhere to.

After a few hours they emerge and, at the next big meeting, announce the company values. They might even have some posters done.

Then, after a few months, they wonder why nothing has changed.

You cannot tell somebody what to value. Values come from within. Which takes me beautifully on to my pet subject, 'happiness'. Please sit up and prepare to be shocked at the next sentence.

You've been conned!
In fact, we've all been conned!

And we continue to con the young people coming through the system!

We are sold a vision of 'happiness' as a desirable pot of gold that lies at the end of the emotional rainbow. By that, I mean happiness is something we have to work hard for. Something to pursue. And we've all fallen for the big fat fib. We tell kids that if they work hard at school they will get great grades and then they'll be happy. And then you'll get a job and you'll have a sales target. And when you hit your sales target, guess what, then you'll be happy. Or you'll be happy when you're walking down the aisle with your perfect partner.

And the truth is that 'happiness' is a fantastic pot of emotional gold at the end of the rainbow. But what if it's not at the far end? What if it's at our end? What if it's not the result of getting great grades but, rather, it's the key to getting great grades? What if it's the happiest kids that do best at school? What if it's the most upbeat and happy sales person that attracts the most customers and effortlessly achieves their targets? What if being happy NOW is the key to finding your perfect partner?

I'll round off this chapter with a very big thought indeed.

What if we've been looking for happiness in the wrong place?

The credit crunch was biting so Eddie decided to give something that was free.

'If you can't explain it simply enough, you don't understand it well enough.'

Albert Einstein

Chapter 8

YOUR BEAUTIFUL MIND

In which we look at the wonders of the world
before going on a polar cruise. We conjure images of
a monkey in a nappy and we end up examining how to get
horses weaned off Hawaiian pizza.

The seven wonders of the world…

A group of school children was asked to list the 'seven wonders of the world'. Although there were some disagreements, the following received most votes:

1. The Great Pyramids of Egypt
2. Taj Mahal
3. Grand Canyon
4. Panama Canal
5. Empire State Building
6. St Peter's Basilica
7. The Great Wall of China

While gathering the votes, the teacher noticed that one quiet student was still working. She asked the girl if she was having trouble with her list.

The girl replied, 'Yes, a little. I couldn't make my mind up because there are so many.'

'Well,' said the teacher, 'tell us what you have and maybe we can help.'

The girl hesitated and then read: 'I think the great wonders of the world are…

1. To see
2. To hear
3. To touch
4. To taste
5. To feel
6. To laugh
7. …and to love.

Your mind is a beautiful thing. But, oh boy, it's also very complex. Let's start with some instructions and information on how you operate. (Don't worry, we're going to keep things as simple as possible.) The first thing you need to understand is that you have a conscious and unconscious mind. They are, metaphorically speaking, similar to an iceberg. There is a part of which we are aware and we call this the conscious mind. This is the tip of the iceberg.

Then there is the part of which we are less aware, and we call this the unconscious mind. In terms of the iceberg analogy, this is beneath the surface. And it's huge! (Just ask the captain of the *Titanic!* In fact, that's not a bad analogy as it's often the unconscious mind that sinks us!)

The job of the conscious mind is to register what you are thinking of right now at this moment in time. It's your awareness. For example, 'I love the iceberg analogy', or 'I fancy a cup of coffee', or 'How did he know I fancied a coffee?' Whatever it is, that is your conscious mind at work. The other job of the conscious mind is to give your unconscious mind direct instruction.

The conscious mind is quite limited in what it can do. Most conscious minds like to think they are very important, but in that respect they are a bit like traffic wardens (a bit of a generalisation there, no offence meant. It's a cheap gag. I'm sure there are some really wonderful traffic wardens in the world. Just not the ones I've encountered.) The conscious mind is also very logical. It likes things to make sense. If things don't make sense, your conscious mind will simply fill in the blanks for you, based on its best guesstimate.

Your unconscious mind runs your body, it keeps your heart beating, liver and kidneys working, in fact all your organs and bodily functions. Have you ever sat there and thought consciously, I'd better keep breathing or I'd better make sure I keep my heart beating tonight while I sleep? Hopefully not – it's all done for you by your unconscious mind.

The unconscious mind is the source of all your emotions as well as filing away all your memories. Everything that has ever happened to you is stored in your unconscious mind. It tries to be helpful by storing it in the form of a line which NLP boffins call a 'timeline'. This enables you to distinguish, and compare, what happened yesterday from what happened to you 10 years ago. If it were not stored in a line we would be aware of our past, but would have no idea of when a particular event had happened. In the interests of simplicity, I won't go any deeper into this but there are some excellent books and articles recommended in the Back of the Book section.

We mentioned earlier that the job of the conscious mind is to give instructions to the unconscious mind, so one of the jobs of the unconscious mind is to carry out these instructions. The unconscious mind does this job to the letter. However – and this is key – the unconscious mind does not process negatives. So if I say to you, 'Don't think of a monkey in a pink nappy' – what pops into your mind? Damn it! A primate in a pink huggie! You cannot manage to not think of something. A favourite one of ours is to say, 'It's impossible to lick your elbow'. Everyone, like you right now, is desperate to give it a go. I know that the urge will overwhelm you and that you will now be gurning your tongue towards your elbow in a vain attempt to make contact. If you're of a more serious nature you will resist for a while but will have attempted to lick your elbow before the day is through. (If I were you, I'd just get it out of the way right now, even if you're reading this on a train.)

This inability to process a negative is one of the main reasons people attract the things they are trying to avoid into their lives. Essentially, most people are constantly telling their unconscious mind what they don't want.

'I don't want to be poor.'
'I hope I don't put on weight.'
'I don't want to be single any more.'

Think of the golfer who says, 'I don't mind where the ball goes as long as it is not into the water.' What follows? *Plop!* This is why it is so important for you to take control of your conscious thoughts, because what you focus on or think about the majority of the time is what your unconscious mind goes to work on attracting into your life. It works like radar. Yet, like a five or six-year-old, it cannot distinguish between what's good for your life and what's not, it just follows instructions. Some people say they think negatively because their lives are rubbish.

Wrong. Their lives are *rubbish* because they think *negatively!*

Let me share an example with you. I live near a man who owns some horses. It just so happened that the school bus stopped right at the gate to his horses' field and, while he was at work, the school children would feed them their scraps. And the gee-gees loved it! Mars Bars, crisps and stuff the kids had made in cookery class. The horses developed a taste for pepperoni pizza! Over time, the horses got fat. So the man put up a sign that said 'Do not feed the horses.'

Did it work? Did it heck! The feeding frenzy continued, so the owner changed the sign. It now read 'Please do not feed the horses!' His problem continued until I bumped into him at a school fête. He knew I was a positive psychology enthusiast so explained the problem in the hope of getting a simple solution. 'How on earth can I stop the kids feeding my horses?'

I chuckled and wrote him a few words on a scrap of paper. The man looked at the paper and laughed. 'No way!' I smiled a knowing smile and the problem was cured. The horses are now back to their normal weight, their coats shining and energy restored. If you saunter past their field there is now a sign that says, 'We only eat apples and carrots'.

The message is simple and positive. It focuses on what we want to happen rather than what we don't want. And, best of all, it works.

Ultimately, this whole book is about language. Get the communication right and the results will follow. Remember, of course, that the most important person you ever communicate with is yourself!

A modern prayer:

'Dear God, help me to slow down

andnotrushpasteverythingthatisimportanttodayamen.'

*From Robert Holden, **Success Intelligence** (2005)*

Chapter 9

NELLIE BREAKS FREE

In which we sneak in a diagram, you run for your life while out shopping, an elephant can't be bothered to escape and some primates fail to evolve.

I'd like to escape, but I'm performing in 40 minutes

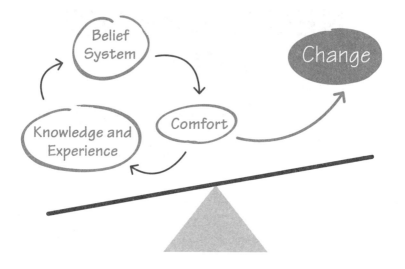

The diagram above illustrates our simplest way of representing some of the key themes of this book. We all live within multitudinal layers of comfort zones. There's part of your mind called your 'reptilian brain' whose sole purpose is to keep you safe. It does all the fight or flight stuff and, in extreme circumstances, it can switch off the rest of your brain.

Let's take an example. Assume you venture into your local city centre on a Saturday evening, intent on some late night shopping. You come across a gang of drunken teenagers who abuse you and threaten you with a broken bottle. I guarantee that your reptilian brain will take over.

You will have an immediate adrenaline rush that pumps energy to your main muscle groups. Your reptilian brain will give you two choices. Fight…but there are ten of them, they've got a bottle and they're drunk. Or flight. So, you run like hell. Your reptilian brain makes sure there's enough adrenaline pumping for you to run faster and further than you've ever run before. And as you sprint past the shop window – where they're displaying the very thing that you popped into town for – your reptilian brain doesn't allow you to stop and think, 'Mmm, nice colour. I'll just pop in and buy that while I'm passing.' No, siree. You run, without even noticing.

This is an extreme fight or flight example. Most of the time your reptilian brain is content with keeping you safe, in the widest sense of the term. So you don't cross roads when lorries are coming, for example. The reptilian brain equates 'safe' with habits, routine and repetitive behaviours.

So, most people get into a routine. The alarm goes off at the same time every morning and they (and their family) go through the same routine. There's an order in which people go into the bathroom. We sit in the same seat, munching on the same brekky cereal, slurping the same tea/coffee with the same milk/sugar. We drive the same car, listening to the same radio station. We have a favourite newspaper and favourite drink, often drunk from our favourite cup. There's even been some interesting research into why people have a 'favourite cup'. It seems that drinking isn't just about taste. It's about a feeling. And your 'favourite cup' enhances the experience.

We're not suggesting there's anything wrong with these habits. They're there to give us routine and make us feel safe.

But the habits also infiltrate our thinking. Negativity and pessimism can easily get a foothold and the way we think can become our downfall. Our comfort zones can restrict us. Comfort zones and habits come from our knowledge and experience.

Crucially, our knowledge and experience determine our 'belief system', and this is the most powerful anchor of all. Our belief system is a deep-rooted view of the world. It manifests itself in the way we speak, think and behave.

Back to the diagram. Most people, most of the time, travel in a circle around the loop. Our brains are brilliant at proving us right. Allow me to borrow a story from Jack Canfield. It's about an elephant, but we think you'll get the point.

There was an elephant who travelled with a circus. The owner figured that the elephant was one of the main attractions so he always positioned it at the entrance to the big top. All the children had the thrill of lining up and feeding the elephant on the way in. Except, of course, you can't just let the elephant loose. It has to be tethered. So, if you look closely, you'll see that the four ton beast has a rope around its ankle. And the rope is tied to a tent peg. And the tent peg is hammered into the grass.

Let me revise the scenario. You have a four ton animal with a rope around its ankle, tied to a tent peg. It's been raining so the tent peg isn't hammered into the ground. The elephant keeper has just pushed the tent peg into the soft turf with the palm of his hand. 'There, that should hold you.'

Why doesn't the elephant do a runner? Why doesn't it take a look at the flimsy and inadequate tether and disappear to Tesco to get some sticky buns?

The answer is, of course, that the elephant is comfortable. It's being fed and watered. It's got a routine. And besides, it doesn't think it can escape. When it was a baby elephant it had a chain wrapped around its ankle. And the chain was padlocked to a lamp post. So, no matter how hard it tried to escape, it just resulted in a sore ankle.

Now the elephant has grown up. It has learned that it can't escape. Its knowledge and experience is that it tried to escape but was trapped. So, what's really holding the elephant back? The rope? The keeper? The fact that it's getting fed every night?

No. The elephant's belief system is what's stopping it. The rope is a symbol. The elephant is an example of what Martin Seligman (2003) calls 'learned helplessness'. The next sentences are difficult to phrase. Without wishing to sound derogatory, are you that elephant? Is there something in your belief system that's holding you back?

To change, we need to go beyond behaviour. Allow me to refer to the brilliant Richard Wilkins once again. He puts it thus: 'You don't change the tide by standing in the ocean. To change the tide you need to go to the moon.' Basically, you don't change behaviour at the level of behaviour. We need to change people's belief systems.

This book is a good example of what I'm talking about. We can't order you to be happy and positive. But if we can get you to believe that by being happy and positive you will have a brilliant next 50 years, then our job is done.

But this is the deep-rooted subconscious image of who you are. So it's not the easiest thing in the world to change. Good news though, it's eminently do-able!

Monkey Management

There were five monkeys who had lived together for some time in a large cage in a municipal zoo. One day their keeper changed.

The new keeper decided to try and dissuade the monkeys from eating their food at the end of the cage farthest from the general public. So when some of the monkeys tried to do this he hosed all of the monkeys with cold water. Quickly the monkeys realised that taking the food to the far end of the cage led to an uncomfortable soaking, so they avoided doing so. Any monkey who attempted to take their food there was quickly and violently apprehended by the others.

Gradually the monkey population aged and changed. Some died, others were moved, a few were brought in from outside. Eventually there were none of the original monkeys left. One day the newest arrival grabbed his food and made for the far end of the cage. The others, seeing what was happening, pounced on him, shrieking and biting and dragged him away.

The new monkey, badly shaken by the ordeal, eventually recovered himself and asked why he had been stopped from eating where he wanted. He was told: 'That's the way we've always done things around here'.

1. How might the above relate to your organisation?

2. Which habits – perhaps habits of mind – do you or your organisation have which are most cherished?

3. Which of these are you willing to give up in order to achieve what you want?

4. True or false: 'If you do what you've always done, you'll get what you've always got.'

5. What three things do you need to start doing

(or doing more of)? What would be the benefits to you and those around you?

6. What three things do you need to stop doing (or do less of)? What would be the benefits to you and those around you?

'Semper in faecibus sumus sole, profundum variat'

Translation: 'We're always in the shit, it's just the depth that varies.'

Chapter 10
LIFE THROUGH A LENS

In which we start off in the doo doo, understand why we always get what we're looking for, introduce 'limbic locking' and find out how to double the cost of getting into Wales.

Once again, in the interests of simplicity, let's give it to you straight. One of the rules of life is that you get what you focus on. I know, I know, it's easy to pick that message to pieces. A guy from last week's course said, 'Oh yeah, so if I focus on the lottery I'm going to win it.' Chortle.

Unfortunately, the principle isn't quite as accurate as that! It's more of a philosophy than a hard and fast 'rule'. Your mind has a wonderful piece of kit called a RAS (that's your Reticular Activating System in case you're interested). The purpose of your RAS is to bring things from your subconscious mind into your conscious mind. Example, I recently travelled to a conference with a lady who's obsessed with nice cars. Now I'm not a car person (as you would know if you saw my beaten-up Mazda, filled with crisp packets and Ginsters wrappers), but every so often the conversation came to a halt as she said, 'Crikey, did you see that Porsche. A silver Carrera. That'll be like the one Clarkson tested in series 4.'

I'd missed it completely.

A few minutes later, 'No way, that was a 4.5 litre Merc CLX! The new one. I can't believe anyone would buy that when you can get the new BMW9 twin turbo soft top for only 5 grand more. Did you see it?'

'Err, no.'

We're driving along the same road, looking out of the same windscreen, yet seeing the world differently. She's focused on cars and that's what she's seeing. I'm focused on getting to Birmingham so am seeing signposts. We're tuned differently. Our RASs are bringing different things to our attention. I guess this begs the question, are you tuned in to the negative or positive in life?

One more example while I'm at it. A guy turned up late on a course last week. He stumbled in without an apology. He mumbled about terrible traffic (although everyone else had made it on time). The coffee and Jammy Dodgers had run out. Not good. He missed the first half hour so was struggling to get the gist of what 'The Art of Being Brilliant' was all about. I was going to catch up with him at break time but he spent 15 minutes on his mobile, shouting to a colleague about a crisis at work. The seats were uncomfortable so he had to stand up for a while. Ironically, he told the group he'd heard many of the messages before so flitted in and out of the group work. He left his moby on because there was urgent stuff back at base. He only asked one question all day and that was 'What time do we finish?' I was interested in his feedback sheet. He rushed off and left it on his seat. In answer to the question 'What can we do to improve the quality of your learning experience?' he'd written 'The drier in the gents doesn't work.'

Thankfully I'm able to laugh about such people. You see, he's not wrong. He's absolutely right! He got exactly what he was looking for. In his world, everything's negative. He notices the traffic and the chaos at work and the lack of coffee and the faulty drier. He's tuned into negative. It's on his radar. And he never notices the good stuff! And, this is the most important point, his life is almost certainly less fun, joyous and pleasurable than it could be if he changed his focus.

It's a black-and-white life. Life's too damned short to be black and white when you can have widescreen high-definition Technicolor. As human beings we're HD ready. Some people are still using an analogue signal. This restricts their quality and choices.

Daniel Goleman (2003) has coined the phrase 'Limbic Locking' and it's a corker. Andy and I often set a limbic locking challenge at the end of 'The Art of Being Brilliant'. 'Limbic' is a posh word that means 'emotion', so the 'limbic lock' translates as the 'emotional lock'. Our 14-day limbic locking challenge is to emotionally lock as many people as you can into the top 2% bracket. Basically, your objective is to deliberately and consciously create a feel good factor in those around you. Ask yourself, what can I do to inspire people? The answers from delegates are always blindingly simple. 'Smile more,' they tell us. 'Praise people.' 'Listen and spend time with people.' Or how about 'Catch people doing things well, and tell them.'

One of our favourite limbic locking challenges is to carry out regular 'random acts of kindness'. This gives me an opportunity to tell my 'Severn Bridge' story.

Just what can positive thinking do?
I was due to give a talk in Cardiff and had to cross the Severn Bridge. For those alien to such things, this is a toll bridge. The day before the journey, I had decided to pay for myself and the car behind me in my first ever random act of kindness. I was so excited as I set off. In fact, I grinned all the way to Bristol, until I saw the sign for the toll charges. At the time of typing these words, it costs £6.00 to get into Wales! I think that's quite a lot of money to get into Wales. I was expecting it to be about a quid! (Interestingly, there's no charge for getting out.) I swallowed hard and grimaced through the adversity. So what if it was going to be a bit

more expensive than anticipated? The act was still on!

I pulled up to the booth and offered the lady my £6.00. She accepted and the barrier was raised. I scrabbled in my glove compartment and cobbled together another £6.00, offering it to the lady, along with a brief explanation. 'I'd like to pay for the car behind me too,' I beamed.

The lady looked alarmed. An axe murderer would have got a warmer reaction. 'What do you want to do that for?' she asked, almost angrily. I was, after all, holding up the traffic.

'It's a lovely day,' I replied. 'And I want to make someone's day. This is my first ever random act of kindness.'

'You only have to pay for one car,' explained the lady, clearly missing the point.

I explained again. Beads of sweat were forming on my upper lip. Doing someone a good turn was much harder than I'd imagined. The car behind honked in frustration. Not good! This was the guy I was treating to a free trip across the bridge! I wanted it to be a lovely, warm hearted and highly appreciative person, not some impatient sales rep who wouldn't even notice.

I'm proud to say that I stuck to my guns. The lady accepted the additional £6.00 and I sped off, grin fixed. In fact it stayed fixed all the way to Cardiff. I felt great! I'd made someone's day – hadn't I? Either the lady in the booth pocketed the money and went for a drink on me (in which case that's good because she'd be chuckling into her pint of

Brains SA) or the slightly impatient bloke got through for free.

Or, maybe (and this sometimes happens in my wildest imagination) the man in the next car arrived at the booth and the lady explained that I'd already paid for him. And he grinned and paid for the car behind him. And that went on all day, with each driver paying for the car behind in a mass act of good will. A tsunami of humanity. An avalanche of good will. A daisy chain of good deeds (enough similes, I hear you cry; we get the point).

Random acts of kindness take many shapes and forms. I've been experimenting with them for the past year or so. They are such great fun. I've bought a McDonald's for a guy I accidentally queue-jumped. I've baked a cake and brought it into work (even if 'That's a random act of food poisoning,' as the office mood hoover pointed out!) I've let someone in front of me in the supermarket queue. They don't all have to cost £6.00. I mowed my neighbour's lawn when he was on holiday. And I felt great!

Go on, you know you can do more of these things. Our challenge is simply to inspire as many people as you can for the next 14 days. Take responsibility, until positivity becomes a habit.

Examples of random acts of kindness
(at various prices from free upwards)...

Let someone in in the traffic

Pay for someone's car park ticket

Buy some flowers and give them to a stranger

Leave a chocolate bar on someone's desk with a note that says 'Have a lovely day'

Wash your partner's car (in secret)

Empty the dishwasher

Volunteer an hour of your time at your local school to listen to children read

Let someone into the supermarket queue in front of you

Pay for the next person's coffee at Starbucks

Do some shopping for an elderly neighbour. Or, if money's tight, stop by for a chat

Bake a cake and bring it in to work. Or, a healthier option, bring in a huge bowl of fruit

Mow your neighbour's lawn

Give someone a hug (but obviously not a stranger in the park)

Thank your parents

Catch someone giving excellent customer service and tell them

Tell someone that you really like their shoes

Buy a lottery ticket and leave it on your neighbour's car windscreen

Pop a voucher for a spa day through a busy but needy mum's letterbox

'The mere thought hadn't even begun to speculate about the merest possibility of crossing my mind.'

Douglas Adams

Chapter 11

THE 90/10 PRINCIPLE

In which we introduce the science of the bleedin'
obvious and realise that positivity boils down to
choice! And we learn that Harry Potter knows all
about it. We introduce the 90/10 principle and
discover how to get a kick out of delayed flights.

Jim's focus was all wrong

Sit yourself down and concentrate. Furrow your brow if it helps. This book is important but this particular section is THE MOST IMPORTANT BIT.

Andy and I have been researching positive people for just about as long as we can remember. They all have a certain set of characteristics or 'habits'. Six things that differentiate them from 'ordinary' people.

And, of the six things, one stands out as being more important than the rest. It's going to seem obvious when you read it. As we say in our workshops, 'It's common sense, but not common practice.'

Are you ready?

The Number 1 thing that positive people do to make themselves happy, upbeat and full of life is that they (imagine a drum roll at this point, please, and maybe some fireworks…)

Choose to be positive!

I know it seems obvious but I'm going to say it again. Positive people *choose* to be positive!

All the upbeat, extraordinary people we've surveyed have all made a conscious decision to lead positive lives. This conscious choice to be positive and upbeat doesn't make the sun shine or the traffic disappear, but it does put you in a better frame of mind to deal with the rubbish that life inevitably throws at you. I don't live in a house on the hill, like the Waltons. There's no 'Good night Jim Bob' resonating in the evening. I have the same environment, news, weather, traffic and work pressures as everyone else. (Probably worse for Andy W living in Mansfield.)

But, by actively choosing to be positive we are better able to attack the issues with purpose, vigour, enthusiasm and are more likely to come up with solutions. Re-read the Zig Ziglar comment in Chapter 3 if you want a reminder.

You can choose to be positive! Obvious? Yes. Are people doing it? No. Like I said earlier, it's common sense but most certainly not common practice. Another interesting way of looking at the choice to be positive is that it's simple, but not easy. Think about that one

> 'It's our choices, Harry, that show what we truly are, far more than our abilities.'
>
> *Albus Dumbledore in J.K. Rowling, Harry Potter and the Chamber of Secrets (1999)*

for a second and let it sink in. Academically, it's the simplest concept you'll ever hear. Choose to be positive. Of course I can. It's obvious. But it's quite difficult to do. Which is why most people don't bother!

Have a go at the following activity. If it hasn't already, the penny will surely drop…

1. What three words or phrases describe who you would like to be as a person?

2. When you're living the words above, what do you:
   Look like?
   Sound like?
   Feel like?

3. How often are you at your absolute best? (Honestly.)

4. What's stopping you?

5. When looking through the lens of the words in question 1, how would you act in the following situations?

- A team member needs your help when you're busy.
- A team member accomplishes a goal or hits a target.
- You make a mistake.
- You disagree with someone.
- Somebody cuts you up at the traffic lights.
- There's a 20-minute queue at Tesco.
- Your grumpy parents are coming to stay for a week.
- You're camping and it's pouring with rain.

If you've thought this through properly, you'll notice you feel and behave much more positively as a 2%er. Check out the 90/10 Principle in the case study below.

The 90/10 Principle is a general theme around which life is based. As with everything else in this book, we've boiled it down to its bare bones.

- 10% of life is made up of what happens to you.
- 90% of life is decided by how you react to the 10%.

What does this mean? We really have no control over 10% of what happens to us. At some point in your life your car will break down and/or you will get a flat tyre. Someone will cut you up in traffic. You will get stuck in a traffic jam and be late for an appointment. Your children will create a mess. Your washing machine will spring a leak. Some of the people at work will be miserable. You have no control over this 10%. We're back to the rather uncouth phrase from earlier, shit happens!

The other 90% is different. You determine the other 90%. This is where the choice to be positive kicks in. The key factor is your reaction to events that happen around you.

You cannot control a red light, but you can control how you feel about it. You may not be able to control the driver who cuts you up in the rush hour, but you can control your reaction.

Eric was travelling flat out to the steam convention

You cannot control the fact that your washing machine has sprung a leak, but you can control your reaction. In fact, you can choose how to feel and react. I'm not saying it's always an easy or obvious choice, merely presenting you with the fact that it exists. And that it's very powerful indeed.

Think about the following step-by-step example.

You are eating breakfast with your family. Your daughter knocks over a cup of coffee which spills onto your business shirt. You have no control over what just happened but it causes the following chain of events:

- You leap up from your chair because the coffee is hot.
- You curse.
- You scold your daughter for knocking the cup over.
- She breaks down in tears.
- After scolding her, you criticise your spouse for placing the cup too close to the edge of the table.
- A short verbal battle follows.
- You storm upstairs and change your shirt.
- Back downstairs, you find your daughter has been too busy crying to finish breakfast and get ready for school.
- She misses the bus.
- Your spouse must leave immediately for work.
- You rush to the car and drive your daughter to school.
- Because you are late, you drive 48 mph in a 30 mph speed limit. You get pulled over by a traffic policeman!
- After a 15-minute delay and throwing a £60 traffic fine away, you arrive at school.
- Your daughter runs into the building without saying goodbye.
- After arriving at the office 30 minutes late, you find you forgot your briefcase.
- Your day has started terribly. As it continues, it seems to get worse and worse. Everything seems to conspire against you.
- You look forward to coming home. When you arrive home, you find a small wedge in your relationship with your spouse and daughter.

The key question is, 'Why did you have a bad day?'

  A) Did the coffee cause it?
  B) Did your daughter cause it?
  C) Did the policeman cause it?
  D) Did you cause it?

If we follow the 90/10 Principle, the answer is D. You had no control over what happened with the coffee.[19] However, how you reacted in those five seconds is what caused your bad day.

Consider the same scenario but with a conscious choice to be positive:

- Coffee splashes over you. You leap up from the table because the coffee is hot.
- Your daughter is about to cry.
- You gently say, 'Don't worry, it was an accident. There's no real damage done, you just need to be more careful next time. Can you clean up the mess while I change my shirt?'
- Grabbing a towel you rush upstairs to change.
- After grabbing a new shirt and your briefcase, you come back down and the coffee has been mopped up. You look through the window and see your little girl getting on the bus. She turns and smiles before getting on. She waves as the bus pulls away.
- You arrive at work early and cheerfully greet the staff.
- Your boss comments on what a good day you are having. Your team is very productive.

---

[19] Technically, you could do a risk assessment prior to every meal, but if you did, the chances are you wouldn't have a family!

Notice the difference? The same start to the day, but two different outcomes. The key point is to make the link between the 'trigger' (spilled coffee) and your 'reaction' (anger in scenario 1 and calm in scenario 2).

Try to think in terms of 'trigger', 'feeling', 'behaviour' and 'outcome' (this will be covered in more detail in Chapter 12). In the above example the spilled coffee is the 'trigger'. The automatic 'feeling' was annoyance and anger. This resulted in 'behaviour' that was aggressive and irritable. The 'outcome' was a downward spiral to the day. If we understand the 90/10 rule, we can begin to control our feelings and therefore trigger different behaviours and outcomes.

The 90/10 Principle is very simple yet very few people actually apply it to their lives. All the instances in the previous exercise are 90/10 scenarios. Camping in the rain, queuing at Tesco, being cut up in the traffic. We cannot control the event but we're absolutely in charge of how we choose to react. And the top 2%ers react differently. Therefore, they tend to get more positive results and, by spooky coincidence, better lives!

I have been experimenting with the 90/10 Principle. I like to play the role of the sceptic. Can you really choose to feel great when things are going badly? In short, yes! I've proved it to myself. Let me share a very simple example. I was lucky enough to do some work in South Africa and was sitting patiently, waiting for my flight out of Heathrow Terminal 5. Thirty minutes before boarding, there was a 'bing bong' over the tannoy and a chirpy lady announced that the flight to Johannesburg had been delayed for two hours because the air conditioning had broken. All 250 of my fellow passengers charged, en masse, to the BA desk to harangue the bing bong lady. 'What kind of rubbish customer service is this?' demanded one angry man. 'It's a disgrace,' shouted another. 'I won't be travelling British Airways again.'

I smiled knowingly (maybe even smugly) and reached for my book. I couldn't control the air conditioning on flight BA57. But knowledge of the 90/10 Principle meant that I could change how I felt about it. I could choose not to get angry. I could feel great, even when those around me were bursting their blood vessels. And besides, I'd just got to a good bit in my book! It sounds bizarre but I thoroughly enjoyed the delay!

Looking back now, the choice to be positive seems obvious. But I hadn't been doing it for 36 years of my life.

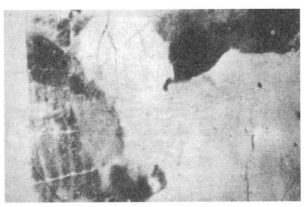

'Picture sourced from Mighty Optical Illusions www.moillusions.com'

Check out the image below and imagine a Rolf Harris voice... 'Can you tell what it is yet?'

The likelihood is that you'll struggle. We've provided a clue at the bottom of the page but the thing is, once you can see it, it becomes fairly obvious. It's rather like the choice to be positive. It's obvious to me now. But only after someone had pointed it out.[20]

----

[20]*You get a lot of them in Jersey, apparently.*

'The best way to cheer yourself up is to try to cheer somebody else up.'

Mark Twain

Chapter 12

TIGGER IS A TRIGGER (AND EEYORE IS TOO!)

In which we introduce the basics of CBT (without even mentioning CBT!), you get to understand the enormity of your impact, we learn the four-minute rule, there's a game of workshop tennis and a cool cartoon about a nun. Plus we visit Elizabethan times and Tom Sawyer teaches you how to get free DIY help.

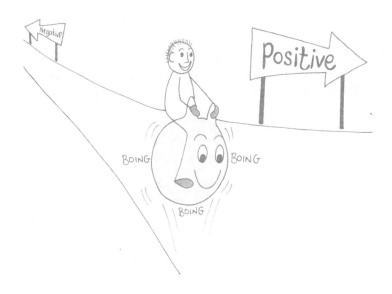

Another very basic rule of human interaction is that you impact on everyone you ever meet. In fact you cannot NOT have an impact. When you walk into a room your presence affects people. Incidentally, I once read an appraisal form on which the manager had written, 'This person lights up the room, when they leave!' Ouch!

This song takes me back to the happiest day of my life...
... my divorce

What we're talking about in this book is the opposite effect. The 2%ers intuitively understand that they're impacting on people and therefore choose, where possible, for that impact to be positive.

We think of it thus:

- Trigger
- Feeling
- Behaviour
- Outcome

There are a million triggers every day. They make us feel a certain way. And our feelings inform our behaviour. And our behaviour determines what happens to us – the outcome. This is a basic model of how your mind works. A classic British trigger is the weather. Let's take a cold, dark, rainy February Monday morning. The alarm goes off and most people crawl out of bed, feeling sluggish and negative, because the weather is awful (again!). So, we feel low. Our behaviour tends to be sluggish and our language negative. There's a lot of huffing and puffing and rolling of eyes. The outcome is that the majority of people have a fair-to-middling day.

Equally, a 'trigger' can be a record that comes on the radio. Music can trigger happiness, sadness, love and holiday memories. Or someone cutting you up in the traffic. The bad driving is the trigger. Our automatic feeling is anger. This leads to aggressive behaviour (in Derby we chase them for three miles, driving 30cm from their bumper, cursing and flashing our lights). The outcome? Road rage. Stress. High blood pressure. Maybe, if we do it on a regular basis, an ulcer.

You are surrounded by triggers. Maybe you've got a picture of your kids on your desk. I used to have some 'lucky pants' that I wore to footy on Sunday mornings. I always scored a goal when wearing my lucky pants and I wore them until they disintegrated. Didn't ever score a goal again!

So, we are subjected to triggers every day. But, get this into your conscious mind, YOU are a trigger. What you say, how you say it, how you walk, how you behave in meetings, what you say when you get home…everything you ever do is triggering feelings in those around you. And those feelings drive their behaviours and determine their outcomes. To reiterate: you cannot NOT have an impact.

Let me tell you a story of how I used to be. My wife and I both work full-time. Louise is a teacher, teaching 11–18s in a comprehensive school. It's hard work and she gets home exhausted. We used to spend half an hour (sometimes a lot longer) bragging about who'd had the worst day. Louise would come in and start moaning about the year 10 'class from hell' and how dreadful the kids are and how she wanted to retire (at age 28!) because she couldn't stick this for another 30 years. But, guess what? I wasn't even listening. I'd heard it all before. I was just waiting for my turn. As soon as Lou paused for breath I was in there. 'You think your day's been bad? Wait till I tell you how bad my day's been…'

It was a daily habit of swapping stories about how grim our days had been. Almost a competition. Focusing almost exclusively on the awful stuff. And, get this, I love my job! So I was drawn into a habit of negativity, without actually realising it. Each of us was triggering a set of negative feelings in the other. The behaviours were often angry, stressed and whingeing. The outcome was a lack of energy. A lifelessness. My wife admitted that 'it was triggering feelings and belief systems in the children, who must have thought work was an awful thing to engage in.' But, like everything, the negativity was just a habit. And habits can change.

Sister Nancy decided to change her habit

Andy and Lou now practise the 'four-minute rule'. This is a long-held principle of HR management but recently popularised by awesome speaker and author of *How to Be a Complete and Utter Failure in Life, Work and Everything,* Steve McDermott.

Steve tells a story of how he sometimes has to work away from home for up to two weeks at a time. On his return journey he would be travelling for hours and his wife would always let his three children stay up to see their dad. He would open the front door absolutely exhausted after an arduous trip and his kids would launch themselves at him shouting 'Dad, it's soooo good to see you!' He would reply with three children hanging off him, often in an exasperated tone, 'Kids, please just let me get through the door. Let me put my case down. Let me get my jacket off. Come on, give me a break, I've been travelling for hours.'

His wife pointed out that in a few years the kids wouldn't be that bothered whether their dad was home or not. This had quite an impact on Steve. On returning from his next trip he thought to himself, 'What would the best dad in the world do when he opened the front door?' So he pretended he was the best dad in the world! He opened the door and dived on the kids, giving them kisses and telling them how great it was to see them. What he noticed is that he only had to do it for four minutes and then the kids got fed up and went off to do other things. Hence the 'four-minute rule'. And we love it!

The principle is that the first four minutes of every interaction are the most important. So, I now go home with the objective of triggering a positive set of feelings in my family. It's a conscious and determined effort to ditch the old habits of whingeing, moaning and griping. I ask my children about the highlight of their day. And I ask them enthusiastically. Then I listen for the answer and engage with them. Getting home has become a thing of joy and smiles. The children no longer retreat to their rooms while mum and dad whinge about their day, sapping each other's energy in the process.

In his book, *The Art of Possibility* (2000), Benjamin Zander talks about 'enrolment', by which he means helping others to make positive choices. We love the term. What can we do to encourage 'enrolment' in the 2% ethos? In the Elizabethan era, gentlemen used to carry a tin containing a smouldering ember. Matches hadn't been invented, so when you wanted a fire, you'd open your tin and use the smouldering ember to light the fire. Once again, the analogy is perfect. We all carry a spark. How many people can we light up (in the nicest possible way, not the pyromaniac kind of way)?

Here's a cool example, taken from *The Adventures of Tom Sawyer* by Mark Twain. There's a classic chapter in which Tom uses the power of positivity to influence his chums. Tom's aunt asks him to whitewash the fence. His friends call by and Tom is seen applying the paint with gusto, pretending to enjoy the chore. 'Do you call this work?' Tom tells his mates. 'Does a boy get a chance to whitewash a fence every day?'

Armed with this new information his friends discover the joys of whitewashing a fence. Before long, Tom's friends are paying him for the privilege as well as deriving real pleasure from the task!

I reckon Tom's a 2%er. He transformed a negative experience into a positive one. He's influenced those around

> him in a positive way. In short, his enthusiasm is infectious. And I reckon there's a message in there for all of us. Whatever job you are attending to right now, choose to do it with passion, energy and enthusiasm. And when you get home, practise parenting in the same vein. You'll feel great – and so will those around you

In *The Tempest,* Prospero called it 'the art to enchant'. In modern times, Seth Godin (2010) calls such people 'Linchpins'. We call them 2%ers. It's the same common denominator; get this right and you will enthuse others with energy and positivity.

Our point in this chapter is about influence and impact. Indeed, it's about the profundity of our influence and impact. And, of course, impact also works in a negative way. My favourite story (and a very painful memory) concerns a delegate called Roy. It was the early days of 'The Art of Being Brilliant' and, while I was full of enthusiasm, I was perhaps a bit wobbly on the research. Someone had clearly volunteered Roy for the course and he was there under duress. Roy was a senior manager in charge of 80 people. He'd got a face like a slapped backside. I bounced into the training room and introduced myself and the course: 'It's going to be a really positive day. In fact, potentially life-changing. Any questions before we start?'

Roy raised his hand and what follows is a verbatim account of the interaction.

'I've got a question,' said Roy.

I nodded in acknowledgement. 'Fire away,' I beamed, rubbing my hands with enthusiasm.

Roy cleared his throat and began. 'What the bloody hell can you teach me?' he asked.

I felt a little crestfallen. It wasn't the best of starts. Roy continued. 'Do I look happy?'

Now I'm an honest lad. I surveyed Roy's 62-year-old face for signs of happiness. All negative. If Roy had a dog it would surely be a bloodhound.

'Er, no,' I replied, truthfully.

The room had gone strangely quiet as Roy continued. 'Let me make this clear before you begin your poxy course. I'm not happy. In fact, I've never been happy,' growled the delegate from Hades. He left a dramatic pause. 'And I've got no intention of starting today.'

It was like a tennis tournament. All eyes were back on me. But no need. The bloodhound was on a roll. 'If I go back to work smiling, they're going to think I'm on something,' he said in a deadpan tone. 'In fact, I've worked here 31 years and haven't had a good day yet.'

My mouth was moving but no words were forthcoming. Blood had drained from my face. Roy pressed on. 'So whatever it is you're going to teach us, I can guarantee I won't be putting it into action. I've got a calendar on my desk,' announced the harbinger of doom, 'and every day, before I go home, I tick off another day. Because it's another day closer to retirement.'

I recovered slightly. Roy's body language indicated that his soliloquy of negativity was nearing an end. 'And anyway,' he said, completely devoid of irony, 'this positive psychology stuff will never work. Because my team's demoralised.'

I can think of some great answers now! Hindsight is such a fabulous gift. But at the time I was left standing at the front of the class, gulping down oxygen like a trout on a hook. I probably tried to look surprised at Roy's revelation. Maybe I looked puzzled. How could it be that Roy's team was demoralised? It'd need a super detective to work this one out. Not!

I survived until break time at which point I did the bravest thing a trainer can ever do. I asked Roy to leave. For everyone's sake it was best he vacate his seat and go and sit next to his calendar.

'The wheel is turning but the hamster is dead.'

Anonymous

The atmosphere lifted and it rates as one of my best

courses ever. I've kept the feedback sheets because one of them has, famously, scrawled on the bottom. 'Best course ever. It's made me realise that I don't want to end up like Roy!'

The learning from Roy's story? Obvious stuff, like why would anyone spend 30 years doing a job they hate? (But many people do.) How can you rise to a senior management position with a belligerent and negative management style that demoralises anyone you meet along the way? (But many do.)

> 'He doesn't have ulcers but he's a carrier...'
>
> *Comment on an appraisal form*

The key learning point is that Roy's team is a reflection of him. Roy was the trigger. In terms of 'mood hoovers' Roy was the 'King Dyson', sucking all the life out of his people, leaving them feeling as demoralised as him. He either didn't know how to inspire people or, even worse, didn't care. He's a perfect example of our second point: 'understand your impact'.

Bottom line? The impact you are having on your fellow human beings is profound. So, if you're going to have an impact anyway, we think you should strive to make it a positive one. Let me set the scene for this awesome quote below. My son plays rugby on a Sunday morning. Kev Brown is one of the dads and also the coach. He, like many other parents, gives up masses of time and is a role model of positivity. He took a minibus of under 10s to Twickenham to watch Leicester v. Wasps, leaving at 10am and getting back at midnight. So I dropped him a quick 'thank you' email and this is the response I got, word for word...

'Thanks Andy

The rugby ethos inspired me when I was young, train hard, play hard, party hard.

If I bring a lifetime love of the game to one child I will be content, many other parents have skills that I could not hope to replicate. When we are old and withered we will have nothing but experiences and memories, most of these are created by the people we come into contact with throughout our lives. I have many failings also, but you are very kind of word.'

KB

He's got it!

I want to finish this chapter with something taken from my previous book, *Being Brilliant.* Not everyone's read it and, even if you have, this part's worth a re-run.

In the grand scheme of things as our planet hurtles through space, spinning on its axis, we are completely and utterly insignificant dots of life flickering on a tiny rock, lost among billions of other tiny rocks in the solar system. On this grand scale our lives are over in the blink of an eye. In this scenario, our insignificance is staggering. But to all those we live and work with (and our children in particular) we are incredibly significant because we form part of their world. We are shaping their character, forming their belief systems and affecting their quality of life. Boy are we significant!

'Dear God

So far today, I've done alright.

I haven't gossiped. I haven't lost my temper.

I haven't been greedy, moody, nasty or selfish.

And I'm really glad about that.

But in a few minutes, God, I'm going to get out of bed.

And from then on I'm going to need a lot more help.

Thank you.

Amen'

From Robert Holden, **Be Happy** *(2009)*

Chapter 13

BEWARE OF THE GARBAGE TRUCKS

In which we learn about bin men, we find out how to date Jennifer Aniston, we liken life to a sausage machine and we go a bit conkers bonkers.

Jeremy's life was full of sh*t

The Law of the Garbage Truck (Pollay, 2010)

How often do you let other people's nonsense change your mood? Do you let a bad driver, rude waiter, curt boss or an insensitive employee ruin your day? Unless you're the Terminator, you're probably set back on your heels. However, the mark of your success is how quickly you can refocus on what's important in your life. 22 years ago I learned this lesson. And I learned it in the back of a New York City taxi cab. Here's what happened.

I hopped in a taxi, and we took off for Grand Central Station. We were driving in the right lane when all of a sudden, a black car jumped out of a parking space right in front of us. My taxi driver slammed on his brakes, the car skidded, the tires squealed, and at the very last moment our car stopped just one inch from the other car's back-end.

I couldn't believe it. But then I couldn't believe what happened next. The driver of the other car, the guy who almost caused a big accident, whipped his head around and he started yelling bad words at us. And for emphasis, he threw in a one finger salute, as if his words were not enough.

But then here's what really blew me away. My taxi driver just smiled and waved at the guy. And I mean, he was friendly. So, I said, "Why did you just do that? This guy could have killed us!" And this is when my taxi driver told me what I now call, "The Law of the Garbage Truck."

He said, 'Many people are like garbage trucks. They run around full of garbage, full of frustration, full of anger, and full of disappointment. As their garbage piles up, they look for a place to dump it. And if you let them, they'll dump it on you. So when someone wants to dump on you, don't take it personally. Just smile, wave, wish them well, and move on. Believe me. You'll be happier.'

So I started thinking, how often do I let Garbage Trucks run right over me? And how often do I take their garbage and spread it to other people at work, at home, or on the street? It was then that I said, "I don't want their garbage and I'm not going to spread it anymore."

I began to see Garbage Trucks. Like in the movie *The Sixth Sense*, the little boy said, "I see Dead People." Well now "I see Garbage Trucks." I see the load they're carrying. I see them coming to dump it. And, like my taxi driver, I don't take it personally; I just smile, wave, wish them well, and I move on.

© David J. Pollay

So far we have two of the 'super six' in the bag. 'Choose to be positive' and 'understand your impact'. The third one is a tad more personal. Let's be clear – the upward arrow from the 'curse of mediocrity' to the 2% zone doesn't happen by accident.

Andy W will never forget being on a Tony Robbins[21] seminar and doing 'your perfect partner exercise'. Basically you imagine your perfect partner and write a list of all their qualities exactly as you want them. Try it, it's really a lot of fun. (I wouldn't recommend you do it in front of your current partner, though.) So there he is, writing furiously, getting very excited about this new lady he's creating. Then came the next part of the exercise, which was simply a question.

'So now, what sort of person do you have to become to attract your perfect partner?'

---

[21] Anthony Robbins: Currently the leading world self-help guru. A bit like Jesus, with millions of followers. Can't walk on water but often walks on fire, which is still quite impressive.

Shock horror! Apparently if you are sat at home in your underpants and vest, drinking Newcastle Brown Ale and eating chips, the chances of Jennifer Aniston knocking on your door and then throwing her arms around you are pretty slim. You have to become someone special to attract someone special. Or, at the very least, be stinking rich.

'What was it that first attracted you to the millionaire Paul Daniels?'

Mrs Merton asks of Debbie McGee

I'd like to... but I can't be bothered

You don't wake up one day magically transformed. It's not effortless. In fact we've gone out of our way to tell you that it is not easy (but very worthwhile) work. It's a bit like getting a six-pack stomach. You can't just turn up at the gym once. 'There we go, that's me done!' You have to work at it. And it's bloody hard work!

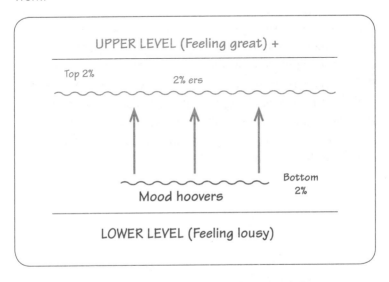

The upward arrow represents a degree of personal change. You do things differently in the 2% zone than you do in the middle and bottom zones. And nobody's going to change your habits for you. YOU have to take charge of it. We call this 'taking personal responsibility' although we could revert to academia and call it 'self-efficacy' or an 'internal locus of control' (but we promised no big words so will gloss over the last sentence!). The 2%ers tend not to blame others. If things aren't working out they are big enough to point the finger back at themselves and say, 'OK, what can I do to get an outcome? How can I change something about me to influence the situation?'

We like Richard Wilkins's analogy of life as a sausage machine. It fits perfectly. We recommend you book yourself onto one of Richard's Broadband Consciousness courses to hear about the sausage machine first hand. Our take on it was based on Jim Collins's 'Good to Great' principle that appeared in Andy C's first book, *Being Brilliant*.

Let's examine the sausage machine. The principle is, as always, deadly simple. Life is about what you put into it. There's a direct correlation between what you put in and what you get out. Richard talks about wanting pork sausages. To get pork sausages, most sane people would agree that they'd have to put pork into the sausage machine in the first place. And if you wanted vegetarian sausages you'd have to put vegetarians in (sorry, I think that should read 'vegetables'!).

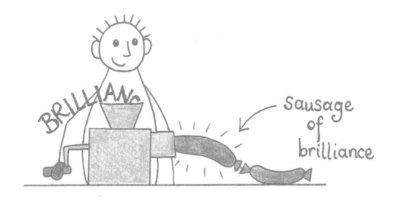

And, just to ram the point home, you wouldn't put pork in and expect vegetable sausages to come out at the other end. That'd be stupid. You'd be waiting a very long time.

So, the point about the sausage machine is to think about what you're putting into life. Are they the right ingredients? Because our point about 'personal responsibility' is that it's your sausage machine and your ingredients. It's not anyone else's! Too many people are putting in low-energy, can't-be-bothered, negativity, whingeing about the bad weather and a perception from the news that the world is going to pot. They stick these kinds of ingredients into their sausage machine of life and wonder why life is dealing them a doom, gloom, low-energy, counting-down-to-the-weekend kind of life. It's a simple rule – garbage in, garbage out.

How about these for ingredients: energy, enthusiasm, confidence, positivity, life, 'can do', exuberance, happiness and smiles. These are just random ingredients that came into my mind. But, I tell you what, you'd have fabulous sausages!

Simple concept. But, once again, not easy to do. Remember, it takes a little bit of effort to be positive rather than negative. And changing habits is the biggest thing of all. In fact, it's backed up by sayings such as 'you can't teach an old dog new tricks', or 'a leopard can't change its spots'. Habits are ingrained. Here are a couple of interesting examples of delegates' habits, gleaned from our work.

One very sceptical lady listened politely and then challenged me. 'OK, Mr Smart Arse Positive Psychologist,' she began (I was guessing she hadn't taken the principles fully on board), 'when I get home tonight,' she said, eyebrows meeting in the middle with a frown that would curdle milk, 'I've got to empty the dishwasher. And I absolutely hate emptying the dishwasher. How, pray tell, am I supposed to empty the f***** dishwasher with enthusiasm and energy when I hate doing it?'

I nodded (hopefully knowingly rather than patronisingly, but it's a fine line). I knew someone would help me out, because the answer was obvious.

'Just be glad you've got a dishwasher,' interjected a voice from the back.

Thankfully there were lots of murmurs of agreement, especially from those who didn't own a dishwasher. 'Or, do it naked,' came another helpful suggestion.

Personally, I'm not sure about the latter (it conjures up all sorts of lewd images that I'm trying to banish from my mind as I type this sentence), but the first point is lovely. And simple. In NLP they'd call it a 'reframe'.

'Look, I don't want to wax philosophic, but I will say that if you're alive you've got to flap your arms and legs, you've got to jump around a lot, for life is the very opposite of death, and therefore you must at very least think noisy and colourfully, or you're not alive.'

Mel Brooks

Of course, it's not easy to empty the dishwasher with passion and energy. But it is possible. Stick the CD player on and sing/dance while you do it. Consciously choose to be positive. And then take responsibility for making the positivity stick.

Another example from a workshop. A guy was rather downbeat. 'I can't be positive,' he claimed, 'because I'm bald.'

What an interesting outlook on life. I explained that you can be cut up about being bald or thankful you've got a head! One will get you low energy, lack of confidence and perpetual doom. The alternative is a joyous, spring-in-your-step, isn't-it-fab-to-have-a-head approach to life. Andy W convinced him it was a solar panel for a love machine which soon changed his approach to baldness.

Now, I always get asked for my conkers story. I told it at a conference (once!) but have never put it in writing before, so here goes.

I've got two children and therefore hardly any spare time. Life revolves around the kids' social lives, taxiing them here, there and everywhere. Getting them to football, swimming, rugby, trampolining, karate or a party. I'm quite posh, so I get *The Times* delivered on a Saturday. And one of my pleasures is to sit and read the paper, not cover to cover, but 20 minutes on a Saturday morning. I always slope off to my middle-class conservatory, put a soothing CD on and then I put my feet up for 20 minutes of relaxation. I'm a sporting nut so my habit is to start the paper from the back page, just in case Derby County have made the news.

Picture the scene. It's late October. A lovely autumnal morning and I've just sat down with *The Times*. Ollie (aged five) bursts in. 'Dad, Dad,' he yells, 'can you come and pick some conkers with me?'

I sigh. It's my quiet 20 minutes and reading the paper is one of my simple pleasures in life. 'Later mate,' I soothe to my youngest. 'I'll pick conkers with you later.'

'But Dad,' pleads Ollie, 'I can't go later because I've got to go to a swimming lesson. We've got to pick conkers now.'

I glance up from my paper. 'I can't go now mate,' I explain, 'because I'm busy.'

Ollie may only be five, but he's not stupid. 'Busy' with your feet up, listening to Enya, reading the paper? So he presses on. 'Dad,' he says earnestly. 'Do you know what conkers are?'

I then struggle to focus on the Sport section while this five-year-old rattles on about how conkers are brown things that hang on trees. And you can have conker fights. And, with all the enthusiasm of a five-year-old, his eyes grow wide when he explains to me that if my conker wins, it absorbs the life of the other conker. Eyes shining, he pushes for a different answer. 'So can we go now?'

Now I think I can outwit a five-year-old. I'm firmly ensconced with my newspaper and am now mildly irritated that my son is stopping my 20 minutes of pleasure. 'Tell you what mate,' I offer, 'when I was your age, Granddad used to let me go and pick conkers on my own. That way it was much more fun.' I settle back to my paper, proud of this fob off. It's classic management textbook stuff. Surely the lad will be empowered to sprint away to the tree and give me the peace I'm craving.

I look up, interrupted yet again, my irritation now growing. Ollie's still there. 'The conkers are too high Dad,' says Ollie. 'I need to go on your shoulders.' And then he's upbeat again as an idea crosses his mind. 'Dad,' he grins, 'we could fill a bucket with conkers and then, when we get them home, we could polish them!'

That's it. I'm now exasperated. I stand up, and fold the paper in half before slapping it down on the table. 'For Heaven's sake,' I spit. 'I can't even get past the Sport section without you whining about conkers. So, yes, we will go and get some conkers. Because otherwise, all I'll hear all morning is "conkers, conkers, conkers" and I won't get any peace until it's sorted. And guess who'll end up cleaning up the mess if you polish them? I've got a million and one other things to do so we'll go and get some conkers but we'll do it quickly…'

Thankfully, Ollie hadn't heard the rant. He'd just heard the 'yes' bit and had scurried off to find his wellies as I whinged to myself.

By the end of the moaning monologue, Ollie had returned with wellies and a white bucket. His grin was huge as father and son set off down the road to the conker tree.

Now spend a few seconds picturing the scene. Ollie is clutching my hand and swinging the bucket in the other. The little boy is singing a song about conkers. He's skipping. Me? I'm slouching. And frowning. Rolling my eyes and thinking how badly I want to finish the paper.

Then, 100 yards down the road, I register the very simple messages in this book, focusing on two principles in particular: the choice to be positive and taking personal responsibility. I realise I'm currently doing neither. I quickly come to my senses and, this is the hard part, change my thoughts. I decide to take personal responsibility for being brilliant and imagine how the best dad in the world would pick conkers and instantly decide to go for it.

Back to the image. It's changed. We now have father and son skipping. I join in the conker song ('conkers, bonkers nuts are we' to the tune of that massive 1980s' hit, 'Snooker loopy') and make up a silly (and slightly rude) second verse. Ollie laughs. The net curtains twitch and the neighbours see two weirdos skipping down the street. They get to the conker tree and I lift Ollie onto my shoulders. To Ollie's delight, some of the conkers aren't quite ready so are white and brown. He's thrilled, shouting out the colours as he adds them to the bucket. Ollie comes down from my shoulders and I throw a stick into the tree. It rains conkers and Ollie scurries like a squirrel, collecting them, filling the bucket to overflowing. There are squeals of excitement as loads of other children join in the fun.

Then homeward bound. Ollie runs the last 50 metres to tell his mum that we've collected 212 conkers. Father and son spend some time deciding on the best 20, which are duly polished, strung up, and I teach my lad the basics of conker fighting. Ollie takes some conkers to school and plays with his mates in the playground.

All in all, the conker episode took approximately two hours. That includes the walk, the gathering, the polishing, making holes, stringing and practice. And, do you know what? I can't think of a better two hours I've ever had![22] All because I chose to be positive and then took personal responsibility for making it happen.

> 'Enjoy the little things, for one day you may look back and realise they were the big things.'
>
> *Robert Brault*

I've only managed to tell this story once, because it's true. And, for some reason, I have to choke back the tears. (Just as I'm doing right now as I write these words!) Why? I'm not absolutely sure but maybe it's because I'm thinking 'how many more years will Ollie want to pick conkers with his dad?'

> 'People think angels fly because they have wings. Angels fly because they take themselves lightly.'
>
> *Anonymous*

---

[22] I know what you're thinking…I should get out more.

Consider the following, written by Nadine Stair, aged 85

I'd dare to make more mistakes next time.

I'd relax, I'd limber up.

I would have been sillier than I have been on this trip.

I would take fewer things seriously.

I would take more chances.

I would take more trips.

I would climb more mountains and swim more rivers. I would eat more ice creams and less veggies.

I would perhaps have more actual troubles but I'd have fewer imaginary ones.

You see, I'm one of those people who live sensibly and sanely hour after hour, day after day.

Oh, I've had my moments and if I had to do it over again, I'd have more of them. In fact, I'd try to have nothing else. Just moments.

If I had my life over, I would start barefoot earlier in the spring and stay that way later in the autumn.

I would go to more dances.

I would ride more merry-go-rounds.

I would pick more daisies.

I've been one of those people who never go anywhere without a thermometer, a hot water bottle, a raincoat and a parachute.

If I had to do it again, I would travel lighter next time. But, you see, I don't get a second chance.

Of course, mood hoovers abound! Garbage trucks are coming at you from every angle. You can almost hear the 'beep, beep, beep' as they reverse towards you, ready to dump their rubbish. The biggest challenge we face is to lock horns with a mood hoover and win. By 'win' I mean we raise their levels of brilliance rather than letting them lower ours!

> 'Encroaching mortality – life is like a party at which guests are randomly taken out by a sniper.'
> *Alain De Botton*

Your best weapon is language. Have a go at the following exercise. It'll help you reframe and rephrase your language in order to begin to fend off the harbingers of doom.

Mood hoover tactics...

Mood hoovers (or energy vampires) need special care and attention. Remember, they have special powers of negativity that can put you under their spell. They make negativity seem so easy – it's so natural. We're like moths drawn to a light.

But we can resist. We have powers of our own. We can even fight back. We all know that garlic repels vampires. The following activities will help you repel mood hoovers. Or, better still, win them over! The first three questions are merely appetisers to get you thinking. They are followed by a series of scenarios that we'd like you to approach from a positive language perspective. Good luck!

1. 'There's no such thing as a sad film.' Agree or disagree? Why?
2. Our natural tendency is to avoid mood hoovers, lest they lower our levels of enthusiasm. Why might avoidance be playing right into their hands?
3. How many mood hoovers does it take to change a light bulb?

Have a go at the following, filling in how you think you could reply in a non-patronising yet positive way. We'll provide an example to get you going. I used to know a mood hoover who would kybosh every idea that was suggested. His catchphrase was, 'That'll never work.' The reframe I used was, 'It's interesting you say that. What do you think would work?'

We're hoping you can see that this simple sentence bounces the issues back to the mood hoover in a way that forces him to come up with a solution. It's not aggressive, patronising or smarmy. Just assertive. Have a go, suggested answers are in the Back of the Book.

What the mood hoover says...	How you should reply...
'It'll never work.'	'It's interesting you say that. What do you think would work?'
'I hate working here.'	
'Nobody has a clue, especially not the management!'	
'Nobody ever listens.'	
'I told you so.'	
'What are you so cheerful about?'	
'Meetings are just a waste of time.'	
'It's just change for change's sake.'	
'I'm just a small cog in a giant machine. I have no impact.'	
'I hate maths, it's sooo boring!'	
'They've forecast another dreadful summer.'	
'Saturday night telly is always rubbish.'	
'Young people today – it's all binge drinking and violence.'	

'It's only when the tide goes out that you learn who's been swimming naked.'

Warren Buffett

Chapter 14
CHUMBAWUMBA

In which we learn that life accelerates as we get older and it can be really shitty at times. We arm you with a 'happy button' and leave you wondering why the chapter title is 'Chumbawumba'.

Positive

Negative

Dear mum and dad

Apologies for taking so long to write, but my writing
utensils were destroyed in the fire at my apartment.
Thankfully I am now out of hospital and the doctor says I
should be able to lead a fairly normal life.

A handsome young man called Pete saved me from the fire
and kindly offered to share his flat with me. He is very kind
and polite so I think you'll approve when I tell you that we got
married last week. I know you'll be even more excited when I
tell you that you are going to be grandparents very soon.

Actually, there was no fire, I haven't been in hospital, I'm
not married or pregnant. But I did fail my biology exam and
I just wanted to make sure that when I told you, you put it
in proper perspective.

Love,
Your daughter

This one's a toughie. Sometimes life can be, how can I put this
gently…really s**t (or, as Andy W would say, 'when the cheese
has slid off your cracker.') The days keep coming at you, thick
and fast. For most people, the weeks are spinning by in a blur.
(I read some research that said life gets faster as you get older,
which stressed me even more because mine's already hurtling
by at a fair old pace. I want to slow it down not speed it up!).
We would be lying if we told you that by choosing to be positive
and taking responsibility for putting superb ingredients into
your sausage machine, every day will be blissful, joyous, happy
and sunny. Andy W's classic story about the birds sitting on your
shoulder and badgers gambolling across your croquet lawns is a
tad Disneyesque.

Let's get real. Even the most positive people have downtime. Everyone can have a bad day. Or a bad week or even a bad month. There are loads of examples of life situations where, quite frankly, it wouldn't be appropriate to be upbeat and positive. I recently volunteered

> '**I bought some Armageddon jam. It said "best before end".'**
>
> *Tim Vine*

to do a talk at my gran's funeral. I tried ever so hard for the words to be positive. To celebrate joyous times and happy memories. The words I'd written were great. The only problem was that I was so choked, I couldn't say them. And, to be frank, if I'd stood at the lectern and beamed from ear to ear it wouldn't have been appropriate. Sniffing the slime back up my nose somehow fitted the occasion. Likewise, even 2%ers have bad days if they're ill or if they lose their job or a relationship turns sour. The good news is that part of being human is to spend some time experiencing negative emotions such as sadness, bereavement, anger, jealousy and frustration.

Yippee! Even happy people get sad!

But not often. They have what we call 'bouncebackability' or what scientists would call 'resilience'. Their habits lie in the upper zone but life will deal them some bad things and they will feel negative emotions. But because their natural predisposition is upbeat, they won't spend an age wallowing in what Paul McGee (2006) calls 'Hippo Time'. It's OK to have a bad day. It's not OK to have a bad life. They will acknowledge the less than perfect situation, allow the feelings to happen and then, after a suitable time, bounce back into the upper reaches of how fab they can feel. 'Bouncebackability' is the hardest of the points. When life's dealt you a redundancy or marriage break-up, or when someone you love dies, then it's very hard to bounce back. The 2%ers manage it, largely because they've chosen to be positive and they therefore know that the current situation is not permanent. They move forward positively rather than wallowing in the negativity. If you like, they remain solution focused rather than problem focused.

> 'You don't get to choose how you're going to die, or when. You can only decide how you're going to live now.'
>
> *Joan Baez*

Andy W lost his mum about two years ago, which most definitely sent him down from the heights of a top 2%er. One of his concerns was breaking the news to Olivia, who was eight at the time and very close to her nan. 'Sorry, Olivia,' he said. 'But we've lost your Nan.'

Olivia looked startled. 'Where, Dad? You can't just misplace grandma!'

'No, I mean we've lost her forever. I'm afraid Nan's died,' sniffed Andy W.

There was a pause from Olivia while she registered the information. 'Is she in heaven?'

'Yes sweetheart. She's in heaven.'

'Cool,' said Olivia. 'She'll love it in heaven. Apparently it's brilliant!'

The lesson? Children can be remarkably resilient!

'There are two ways to live: you can live as if nothing is a miracle; you can live as if everything is a miracle.'

Albert Einstein

People forgot 'Tigger's' real name was 'Derek'

There are various NLP techniques that will help you bounce back. 'Anchoring' is probably the simplest. Once again, in terms of keeping things understandable, we'll provide a quick technique that we sometimes use in the workshops. We call it the 'Happy Button'.

The Happy Button

Read the following passage and then close your eyes and do it. Remember, eyes closed, but mind wide open!

Think of a time when you felt invincible. A time when you felt like you could take on the world. Maybe it was your wedding day (or the day you got divorced!). Or you passed an exam or your driving test. The birth of a child. A presentation that you gave that was awesome. Remember back to that time and run the movie in your mind. Turn up the colours and sounds. Run it forwards, choosing to slow it down at the moments when your brilliant feelings peaked. It's your movie. They are your memories and feelings. This is the Director's Cut.

Now open your eyes and find a felt tipped pen. Draw a circle on the back of your hand. Close your eyes and run the movie again. The same as before but turn the colours up even brighter.

Magnify the feelings. Then magnify them again. Feel the brilliance flowing through you. Confidence. Happiness. Love. Positive. Isn't it great to be alive?

As the feelings reach a crescendo, gently press on the circle. Press just a little bit harder and hold while you run the main event of the movie. Let the feelings flow into your Happy Button.

And that's all there is to it. If this is the first time you have done this kind of thing it may feel a bit weird, but you've just anchored yourself into a positive state. We advise that the Happy Button is pressed in emergencies only. It's not for when the traffic lights are on red – it's for when life deals you some serious stuff and you need a short boost to get through a situation. Or maybe at an interview or to give you confidence before a presentation. It only takes a second. Press the back of your hand and recall the time when you felt 10 feet tall and bullet proof. The good feelings are released and you'll feel much better. But, as I say, emergencies only, please. Don't wear your Happy Button out!

> 'Failure is only the opportunity
> to begin again, more intelligently.'
> *Henry Ford*

'I'm struggling to adjust to my new Bonnie Tyler sat nav. It keeps telling me to turn around and every now and then it falls apart.'

Unknown

Chapter 15
SHARE A HUGG

In which we put the boot into SMART and give you a HUGG instead. An old fellow enrols on a medical degree. Some fatherly advice is dished out, we learn some stuff about the 9/11 rescue operation and finish with a fab story about Clarence and Felix.

Living the dream

A young man was enroling on the first day of his new university course. Stretching ahead were seven years of training that would eventually earn him a medical degree and the opportunity to work in the career he'd always wanted.

As he stood in the enrolment line he sparked up a conversation with an elderly gentleman standing behind him in the queue. Both men agreed that becoming a medic was something they'd always dreamed of. The young man couldn't help commenting on the old man's age. 'If you don't mind me asking,' he enquired, 'how old are you?'"

The old man chuckled. 'I've just turned 73,' he replied proudly, standing tall and breathing deeply.

The young man looked amazed. 'But that means that in seven years' time, when you qualify, you'll be 80!'

The old man beamed again. 'Young fellow,' he said, 'in seven years' time I'll be 80, whether I live my dream or not.'

If you've ever been on a management course, you'll be familiar with goals. Probably SMART ones (and, no, I'm not going to trot out the words behind the acronym. Other books will go there. We're avoiding it like the plague.)

We prefer HUGGs. These are Huge Unbelievably Great Goals. HUGGs are whopping goals, on the edge of achievability. You'll need to stretch yourself to attain them. You won't achieve your Huge Unbelievably Great Goal by sitting watching *Eastenders* (unless your goal is to watch every episode of *Eastenders*, in which case you've got a remarkably sad life).

It's all about having some direction. If you don't set yourself a target you have no chance of reaching it.

Sylvia decided to test herself with
a climb of 'Mediocre Mountain'

Andy W recalls that when he left school, he didn't set himself
a target or even give it much thought. 'I just did what a lot of
people do. I drifted.' He ended up following his father's advice,
'Join the army son, you will see the world,' and spent the next
three years in Reading running around a field with a bush on his
head at 5a.m. every morning. 'Thanks Dad!'

Andy W always tells people to 'aim for the sky and if you miss
you'll end up amongst the stars.' He can be really cheesy at
times. And, speaking of cheesy, check out the following quote.

'How can you say, "the sky's the limit" when there are footsteps on the moon?'

Anonymous

Raymond had begun his Mr Universe quest

It's a curious British trait that many people say they don't want to aim too high because if they don't reach their goal they will be disappointed. We're back to the British mentality of setting low expectations in life. That way, if something good does actually happen, it's a bonus! We're amazed at how many people have that philosophy of life. They are aiming for averageness!

The secret to setting HUGGs is that they should excite you. It doesn't matter if it's a personal goal, team goal, career goal or family goal.

It can be anything from getting your book published to running a marathon to being the best mum in the world to getting a degree or looking great in your swimming trunks.

Close your eyes and picture yourself having achieved your goal. Wow! What do you see, hear and feel?

There's an awful lot of nonsense written about goal setting. David Taylor demystifies it in his brilliant book, *The Naked Leader* (2002). David distils it down into the following four stages:

1. Work out where you are now
2. Work out where you want to be
3. Work out what you have to do to get there
4. Do it!

Wow! Have you ever read anything so brilliantly simple?

David Hyner introduced me to his goal setting pyramid some years ago. David is the guru of goal setting. His system is simple and, best of all, it works. I used it to move forward on my HUGG of getting my first children's novel published, *Spy Dog*.

'Dreams come true; without that possibility, nature would not incite us to have them.'

John Updike

Check out the following pyramid. The HUGG goes in at the top and you then work from the bottom upwards. Fill in the blocks with the things you are going to do to move you towards your goal. Rocket science it ain't. Brilliant, it surely is.

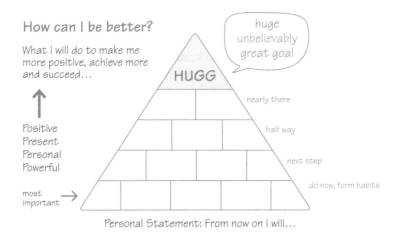

How can I be better?

What I will do to make me more positive, achieve more and succeed...

HUGG

huge unbelievably great goal

nearly there

half way

next step

do now, form habits

Positive
Present
Personal
Powerful

most important →

Personal Statement: From now on I will...

Of course, we're all familiar with the concept of setting goals. New Year's Eve is the classic goal-setting occasion. It's a very simple principle. Fact – gym membership shoots up by 50% in January. Most people never visit the place again after February! Like everything in life, it takes effort. And if there aren't some quick wins we can become jaded. Enthusiasm wanes all too quickly.

Check out this example, which is both heart-warming and heart-breaking at the same time. There was a team of dog handlers working amongst the 9/11 rubble. Imagine the devastation of the scene. But there remained a faint hope that some people might be buried, but alive. The rescue dogs worked tirelessly, despite blistered and bleeding feet. But they became frustrated. The dogs were trained to sniff out survivors but the reality was they were finding bodies. The dogs were losing their spirit because they weren't achieving their goal. The dog handlers had to hide volunteers in the rubble so the dogs could sniff out living people and regain their enthusiasm.

The moral of this heart-rending story? Maybe it's that we need to build in some rewards along the way. A huge goal (or goals) is the ultimate aim but plant some markers along the way – some points at which you can enjoy a small reward on the road to your huge goal(s).

> 'Vision without action is merely a dream. Action without vision just passes the time. Vision with action can change the world!'
>
> *Joel Barker*

So while we are advocates of huge goals that stretch and excite you, we are also wary of setting targets that are so scary they will kill you! Consider the following story of Clarence and Felix. Their rather sad story also acts as a tasty sandwich filling between this chapter (goals) and the next one (strengths).

Clarence and Felix

The world, from a frog's perspective

Once upon a time there lived a man named Clarence who had a pet frog named Felix. Clarence lived a modestly comfortable existence on what he earned working at Tesco, but he always dreamed of being rich.

'Felix!' he exclaimed one day, 'We're going to be rich! I'm going to teach you how to fly!' Felix, of course, was terrified at the prospect. 'I can't fly, you idiot! I'm a frog, not a canary!' Clarence, disappointed at the initial reaction, told Felix, 'That negative attitude of yours could be a real problem. I'm sending you to college.'

So Felix went on a three-day course and learned about problem solving, time management and effective communication — but nothing about flying.

On the first day of 'flying lessons', Clarence could barely control his excitement (and Felix could barely control his bladder). Clarence explained that their apartment had 15 floors, and each day Felix would jump out of a window, starting with the first floor and eventually getting to the top floor. After each jump Felix would analyse how well he flew, concentrate on the most effective flying techniques and implement the improved process for the next flight. By the time they reached the top floor Felix would surely be able to fly.

Felix pleaded for his life, but his pleas fell on deaf ears. 'He just doesn't understand how important this is,' thought Clarence, 'but I won't let such negativity get in my way.' So, with that, Clarence opened the window and threw Felix out (he landed with a thud).

Next day, poised for his second flying lesson, Felix again begged not to be thrown out of the window. With that, Clarence opened his pocket guide to 'Managing More Effectively' and showed Felix the part about how one must always expect resistance when implementing new programmes. And, with that, he threw Felix out of the window (THUD!).

On the third day (at the third floor), Felix tried a different ploy. Stalling, he asked for a delay in the project until better weather would make flying conditions more favourable. But Clarence was ready for him. He produced a timeline, pointed to the third milestone and asked, 'You don't want to slip behind schedule, do you?' From his training, Felix knew that not jumping today would mean that he would have to jump TWICE tomorrow. So he just said, 'OK, let's go.' And out of the window he went.

Now, understand that Felix really was trying his best. On the fifth day he flapped his feet madly in a vain attempt to fly. On the sixth day he tied a small red cape around his neck and tried to think 'Superman' thoughts. Try as he might, though, Felix couldn't fly.

By the seventh day Felix, accepting his fate, no longer begged for mercy. He simply looked at Clarence and said, 'You know you're killing me, don't you?' Clarence pointed out that Felix's performance so far had been less than exemplary, failing to meet any of the milestone goals he had set for him. With that, Felix said quietly, 'Shut up and open the window.' He leaped out, taking careful aim for the large jagged rock by the corner of the building. And Felix went to that great lily pad in the sky.

Clarence was extremely upset, as his project had failed to meet a single goal that he set out to accomplish. Felix had not only failed to fly, he didn't even learn how to steer his flight, as he fell, like a sack of cement. Nor did he improve his productivity when Clarence had told him to 'Fall smarter, not harder.'

The only thing left for Clarence to do was to analyse the process and try to determine where it had gone wrong. After much thought, Clarence smiled and said, 'Next time, I'm getting a smarter frog!'
(Source: unknown)

1. Look at the world from Clarence's perspective. What is he feeling?

2. Look at the world from Felix's perspective. What is he feeling?

3. How might this story relate to your workplace?

4. Other than 'frogs can't fly', what is the moral of this story?

'Skills: Strong work ethic, attention to detail, team player, self-motivated, attention to detail.'

On work experience application

Chapter 16
STRENGTHENING YOUR STRENGTHS

In which we ask you to be very un-British and look at what you're good at! We discover why eels are top of the class. We learn to go with the flow, learn something interesting from Excel and Ginny runs a marathon, slowly!

Ginny was so good at the shot put that she decided to go for the marathon as well

The animal school

Once upon a time the animals decided they must organise themselves to meet the problems of the new world. So they organised a school.

They adopted an activity-based curriculum consisting of the essentials in life, namely running, climbing, swimming and flying. To make it easier to administer the curriculum, all the animals took all the subjects.

The duck was excellent at swimming, in fact better than his instructor, but he was only average at flying and was very poor at running. Since he was slow in running he had to stay after school and also drop swimming in order to practise running. This was kept up until his webbed feet were badly worn and he was only average at swimming.

The rabbit started at the top of the class in running but had a nervous breakdown brought on by the pressure of having to learn to swim and fly.

The squirrel was excellent in climbing class. She tried to teach the others but over-exerted herself and ended up with a C in climbing and a D in running, failing flying and swimming altogether.

The eagle was a problem pupil and was severely disciplined. In the climbing class she beat all the others to the top of the tree but insisted on using her own way of getting there. The teacher was annoyed that she failed to follow the climbing instructions and her wings were clipped as punishment. Now she couldn't fly at all and was learning to run instead.

At the end of the year an abnormal eel that could swim exceedingly well and could also run and fly a little, had the highest average and was hailed 'top of the class'. He died soon after as a result of an unfortunate climbing accident.

> The dogs stayed out of school and fought the authorities because they wouldn't add digging and retrieving to the curriculum.
>
> (Source: unknown)

The moral of this story ties in with the final of our six points. There has been some exciting research in recent times, led by luminaries such as Alex Linley and Marcus Buckingham around the concept of signature strengths. Once again, we will distil the research into its simplest form (thankfully the information is relatively straightforward anyway).

Basically, you've got a much better chance of feeling fantastic if you're in an occupation where you're given plenty of scope to play to your strengths. You intuitively know this to be true without us having to hammer it home. You know that you come alive when you're challenged in just the way you like to be challenged. You've got skills that someone's recognised and you are bringing them to the fore every day. As Buckingham says in one of his excellent videos, these are times when 'work doesn't feel like work'. It's akin to Csikszentmihalyi's (1991) concept of flow. Time flies. You're totally absorbed in whatever it is you're doing. And you don't feel exhausted. On the contrary, you feel refreshed and invigorated!

So, playing to your strengths makes you come alive! If we know this to be true, why do most organisations send people on courses to plug their weaknesses? Why do we recruit people because of their strengths and then carry out appraisals to find their weak areas?

Take me as an example. As a junior manager I once had a 360 degree appraisal. That means everyone had their say, even my customers! I was summoned for feedback. Yikes! I'm proud to say that most of it was glowing. I was rated very highly in 24 of the 25 categories. I sat there grinning. 'But,' my manager confided, 'the weak area is spreadsheets. You obviously don't know how to use Excel,' he said, pointing at the evidence in the report.

'Ex what?' I said. I'd never heard of it. I was a trainer so didn't need to use Excel. PowerPoint was my thing.

'Spreadsheets,' he continued. 'They allow you to calculate things. They use them in accounts a lot.'

'Thank goodness I'm not in accounts then,' I chuckled in a pally kind of way. ''Cos my other scores are great.'

> 'It is impossible to live without failing at something, unless you live so cautiously that you might as well not have lived at all – in which case, you fail by default.'
>
> J.K. Rowling

But he couldn't get past the Excel issue. My personal action plan was – you've guessed it – to enrol on an Excel spreadsheets course! Which demoralised me greatly, frustrated the hell out of me and made me sulk like a naughty child.

There's absolutely no doubt that their money would have been better spent developing me in areas where I was already pretty good. I'd have got excited about going on an NLP course. Or some advanced PowerPoint. Or maybe something cutting edge in the pink and fluffy field. Whoopee! I'd have bounced out of my 360 degree review singing the organisation's praises, rather than skulking out like a scolded brat.

Businesses the world over are making the same mistakes. Maybe, just maybe, we can turn conventional thinking on its head. Maybe you will get more value from your training budget by breaking with tradition and spending time and money developing your people in areas they're already good at!

Which, I guess, brings us back to weaknesses. What are we supposed to do about them? Ignore them and hope they'll go away? Err, no. Our advice on weaknesses is to be aware of them. Plug them if they are stopping you performing your job safely or competently. Other than that, chill. Everyone has weaknesses. What you'll find is that successful people focus on their strengths rather than their weak areas. In fact, often they succeed despite their weaknesses. (For example, did you know that Richard Branson is dyslexic?)

Remember Clarence and Felix from the previous chapter? The poor frog who came to a sticky end because he couldn't learn to fly. It was a ridiculous goal for a frog. But it's amazing what can be achieved if we set goals that play to people's strengths. Setting Felix a target to leap higher or catch more flies with his sticky tongue would have played to his amphibian strengths. Felix would have strived to succeed. He would have been focused. And, crucially, he would have been motivated rather than dead!

We'll leave the final word in this chapter to Alex Linley (2008) and what he calls 'the curse of mediocrity'…

Who wants to be average?

The curse of mediocrity is all around us. In our education systems we see it in the perennial quest to have every student being good at every subject. They are not.

At work we see it in well-meaning competency models, where everyone is expected to be good at everything. They are not, and this being so, we then focus on what is wrong and what isn't working, trying to fix the weakness.

In the world of psychology we have seen it in the focus on treating disease and overcoming psychological illness; laudable aims in themselves of course, but aims that will never move people beyond the zero point of being 'not ill', rather than being 'really well.' …

When we try to ensure that everyone is good at everything, we are condemned by the 'Curse of Mediocrity.'

Alex Linley, *Average to A+* (2008)

1. What is your gut feeling about Linley's observations?
2. What is your vision for a successful life? Describe a life well lived.
3. What is your vision for your relationships? Describe the sort of friend/partner/parent/son/daughter you want to be.

4. What is your vision for your work? Describe the contribution you want to make.
5. What kind of person do you want to be?
6. Think back to a time when you were allowed to play to your strengths. What happened and how did you feel?
7. 'You learn most in your areas of strength.' True or false? Why?
8. Is it possible to play to your strengths in the modern workplace?
9. What are the key learning points from this exercise?

'Dance with life and you'll soon get everyone else dancing!'

Anonymous

Chapter 17

OMNIPOTENT HANDSTANDS

In which we visit Seb in Lane 10, live the length and breadth of life, sum up our six points and end with the best nested loop ever.

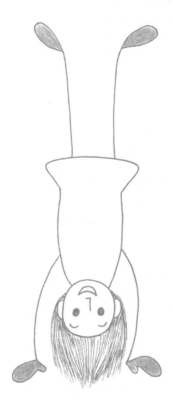

One of our absolute favourite stories pertains to the quote that opens this chapter. Like everything else we do in 'The Art of Being Brilliant', its genius lies in the simplicity of the story. Is it true? Not sure. We can't even remember where we read it. But it sounds as though it could be true. Enjoy…

There's a toll bridge, somewhere in America. Let's imagine it's somewhere sunny and warm and there are 10 lanes of traffic. It costs a couple of dollars to cross the bridge and, to be honest, taking the money isn't the most inspiring of jobs. The toll collectors spend their shift cooped up in a small cubicle, taking the $2 and pressing a button to lift the barrier. It's repetitive and monotonous. Understandably, most employees go through the motions. They are zombie-like, wishing their time away.

Except one. In Lane 10 we have a guy called Seb. And Seb loves coming to work. In fact, he brings his CD player and parties for the entire eight-hour shift. He pumps up the volume. He often manages a dance, too (despite the confines of his cubicle). And there's always a grin, one of those ear-to-ear grins that lights up his whole face. Sometimes a comment too. After all, Seb knows quite a few of his regulars.

'Have a great day, Mr B.'
'Say "hi" to the kids, Marianne.'
'Welcome to Lane 10. Isn't it a glorious day?' he grins at the next customer.

The bottom line is that Seb loves coming to work. He's made

a conscious choice to feel great. The zombies in Lanes1–9 take the customers' cash with anodyne efficiency. They wish they weren't there. Lane 10 stands out a mile!

And here's the rub – if you cross the bridge after the rush hour's subsided and the queues have dwindled – you will notice a strange phenomenon. Lanes 1 to 9 are empty. The zombies are strumming their fingers. You can drive through in an instant. And Lane 10 has a queue. Seb has his devotees. These are people who would rather queue for five minutes to pay their $2 to Seb than breeze through Lanes 1–9.

I'll leave the final thought as a question. Why do you think these busy commuters would rather spend five minutes queuing at barrier number 10?

If you can figure this one out, then this book's been a worthwhile read.

'I don't want to get to the end of my life and find that I just lived the length of it. I want to have lived the width of it as well.'

Diane Ackerman

Now you've read our book you have enough information, if you put it into practice, to move you into the top 2% bracket. You can join the merry band of 'happy people'. You've got a better chance of having a better life.

> The six points are yours for the taking. Let's revise them:
> 1. Choose to be positive.
> 2. Understand your impact.
> 3. Take personal responsibility.
> 4. Have bouncebackability.
> 5. Set Huge Goals.
> 6. Play to your strengths.

> 'Change will not come if we wait for some other person or some other time. We are the ones we've been waiting for. We are the change that we seek.'
>
> *Barack Obama*

Is there anything above that you cannot do? Or anything dreadfully complex that you can't fathom?

No? Then may we respectfully ask that you go and do them? It just takes a little effort.

…Beads of sweat gathered on my brow. 'Can God do a handstand?' It's a sublime question. I didn't want to venture into the ridiculous so I needed a great answer. This innocent drive was turning out to be quite a challenge. I'm not sure I even believe in God! If I did believe in him, would he be able to do a handstand? I could picture the old fella, up there somewhere, sitting on a cloud, or throwing bolts of lightning down at us. Sure he was wise. Omnipotent even. But athletic? I'd never considered God to be athletic.

The motorway hummed by. I checked Olivia in the rear view mirror. She was waiting for my answer. God's old, right? If my Sunday school teacher was right, he's been around pretty much since the dawn of time. Maybe even longer. But what was there before the Earth was there? My mind was wandering. What preceded the Big Bang? I missed my exit and came to my senses. I reckoned God could probably do a forward roll. And possibly a star jump. But a handstand? My eyebrows met in the middle and I swerved to avoid a lorry. After great deliberation I answered Olivia's question.

'Can God do a handstand? You know something sweetheart?' I said, glancing at my beautiful little girl in the rear view mirror. 'Probably not!'

I glanced in my rear view mirror. Was this the right answer? A big smile appeared on her face as she replied in a very confident manner. 'Well, Daddy, if he comes round our house I will show him how it's done.'

My eyebrows no longer met in the middle. They were raised in surprise. 'If he comes round our house I'll show him how it's done!' Was my little girl really willing to teach God how to do a handstand? How fantastic is that! And what a superb example of sharing best practice.

Or 'if he comes round our house I'll show him how it's done.' Was my little girl challenging God to a head-to-head handstand competition round the back of a three-bed semi in Mansfield? My little girl against the omnipotent creator of life. If that's the case, whatever challenges we face seem feeble in comparison!

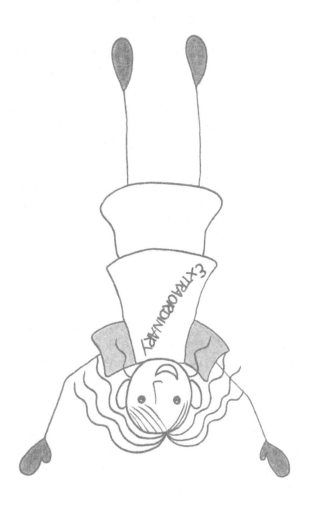

Back of the Book

Suggested answers to exercise in Chapter 13

1. 'There's no such thing as a sad film.' Discuss

An interesting technical point. If you ever study 'NLP' (which we think you probably should as it has plenty of merit, despite some serious drawbacks), you'll become accustomed to the fact that 'there's no such thing as reality'. Now, I don't want to scare you and suggest there's a *Matrix*-style parallel world going on around us – but there actually is![23] Think of the saddest film you've ever seen (let me guess, *Bambi*?) and what you'll find is that the movie is a series of images and sounds that we attach an emotion to. Basically, the film is neutral. The 'sad' bit comes from our interpretation.

2. Our natural tendency is to avoid mood hoovers, lest they lower our levels of enthusiasm. Why might avoidance be playing right into their hands?

Phew! A lot easier to explain than the previous point. Our natural defence mechanism is to avoid mood hoovers. There are negative people at work whom we know will lower our levels of enthusiasm so we only interact with them if we absolutely have to. Understandable. We want to stay sane! The problem is that this tactic of self-preservation doesn't actually tackle the problem. The mood hoover is allowed to wallow in their negativity. They remain untackled. They are free to spread their bad vibes and to sap the energy of your innocent co-workers. Case in point, a genuine mood hoover conversation overheard yesterday: elderly employee discussing whether he should take voluntary redundancy. 'But no,' he concluded. 'I really enjoy coming to work for a moan.'

3. How many mood hoovers does it take to change a light bulb?

Your answer may be better than ours. We think the answer is none. They'd prefer to whinge about working in the dark rather than changing the bulb. Plus, it'd be against Health and Safety to change it anyway!

We've provided some suggestions to the mood hoover conversations that we all get drawn into. The easiest thing is either to get angry or, even worse, join in with the mood hoover's negative ethos. So we've provided two sets of answers – the things you'd like to say versus the things you really should say.

----

[23] *Hands up if you actually understood the Matrix triology?*

What the mood hoover says...	How you'd like to reply	How you should reply...
'It'll never work.'	'Nice one Einstein. Now you tell me!'	'It's interesting you say that. What do you think would work?'
'I hate working here.'	'And we hate having you here. Here's the jobs page. Check it out.'	'That's unfortunate. What do you think you can do to enjoy it more?'
'Nobody has a clue, especially not the management!'	'Too bloody right. Couldn't organise a piss up in a brewery.'	'Interesting. So if you were in their position, what would you do?'
'Nobody ever listens.'	'That's because all you ever do is whinge.'	'How do you think you can make your points in a positive way so they will take them on board?'
'I told you so.'	'Yes, but you're always such a misery that we've stopped listening to you. That means that on the odd occasion that you are right, we've discounted your opinion.'	'What ideas have you got to move us forward?'
'What are you so cheerful about?'	'Seeing your cheery smile!' (said with a degree of sarcasm)	'I've made a choice to have a great day. Tell me some stuff you've got to be cheery about.'

What the mood hoover says…	How you'd like to reply	How you should reply…
'Meetings are just a waste of time.'	'Especially when you whinge and moan at everyone else's ideas and fail to offer anything even semi-constructive.'	'How do you think we could organise them better?'
'It's just change for change's sake.'	'You would say that, you stick in the mud. If you had your way we'd go back to the good old days, pre-wheel.'	'What do you think are the consequences of our team standing still?'
'I'm just a small cog in a giant machine. I have no impact.'	'Well p**s off then.'	'Have you ever slept in the same room as a mosquito?'
'I hate maths, it's sooo boring!'	'Yes, but your maths teacher is dead fit.'	'Tell me about how maths might be useful as you get older.'
'They've forecast another dreadful summer.'	'Sod it, I'm emigrating to Dubai.'	'Tell me about the most fun you've ever had in the rain!'
'Saturday night telly is always rubbish.'	'So why do you watch it, muppet?'	'Tell me what else can you do on a Saturday night other than watch telly?'
'Young people today – it's all binge drinking and violence.'	'Lucky b******s!'	'Lucky b******s!'

References

Brilliant, Ashleigh. Author and thinker http://www.ashleighbrilliant.com

Buckingham, Marcus. Speaker, researcher and author http://www.tmbc.com/

Canfield, Jack. Author and speaker http://www.jackcanfield.com/

Collins, Jim. *Good To Great: Why Some Companies Make the Leap... and Others Don't* (2001) Random House Business
http://www.jimcollins.com/

Colsubsidio Book Exchange. Columbian project, now finished. No website

Csikszentmihalyi, Mihaly. *Flow: The Psychology of Optimal Experience* (1991) Harper Perennial

De Botton, Alain. Philosopher, author and broadcaster
http://www.alaindebotton.com/

Ehrenreich, Barbara. *Smile or Die: How Positive Thinking Fooled America and the World* (2010). Granta Books
Author and speaker http://www.barbaraehrenreich.com/

Frankl, Viktor. *Man's Search For Meaning: The classic tribute to hope from the Holocaust* (2004) Rider New Edition

Godin, Seth. *Linchpin: Are You Indispensable? How to Drive Your Career and Create a Remarkable Future* (2010) Piatkus Books
Author, thinker and blogger http://www.sethgodin.com

Goleman, Daniel. *The New Leaders: Transforming the Art of Leadership* (2003) Sphere
Author of numerous books about emotional intelligence
http://danielgoleman.info/

Holden, Robert. Success *Intelligence: Timeless Wisdom for a Manic Society* (2005) Mobius
Speaker and author http://robertholden.org

Hyner, David. Trainer and expert in goal setting
http://www.stretchdevelopment.com

Linley, Alex *Average to A+: Realising Strengths in Yourself and Others* (2008) CAPP Press. http://www.cappeu.com

Lowe/SSP3. Art & Graphics company http://www.lowe-ssp3.com

McDermott, Steve. Author and speaker http://www.stevemcdermott.com

McGee, Paul. *S.U.M.O. (Shut Up, Move On): The Straight-Talking Guide to Creating and Enjoying a Brilliant Life* (2006) Capstone. Speaker and author http://www.thesumoguy.com

Ossowski, Radek. Artist http://megaossa.deviantart.com

Pollay, David. *The Law of the Garbage Truck: How to Respond to People Who Dump on You, and How to Stop Dumping on Others* (2010) Sterling. www.davidpollay.com and www.thelawofthegarbagetruck.com

Pryce-Jones, Jessica. *Happiness at Work: Maximizing Your Psychological Capital for Success* (2010). Wiley-Blackwell

Robbins, Anthony. Motivational speaker and author http://www.tonyrobbins.com

Rowling, J.K. 'The Fringe Benefits of Failure, and the Importance of Imagination', www.harvardmagazine.com, 6 May 2008

Seligman, Martin. *Authentic Happiness; Using the New Positive Psychology to Realise Your Potential for Lasting Fulfilment* (2003) Nicholas Brealey Publishing www.authentichappiness.sas.upenn.edu/Default.aspx

Taylor, David. *The Naked Leader* (2002) Capstone. Author and speaker www.nakedleader.com

Wilkins, Richard. Speaker and self-styled 'Minister of Inspiration'. www.theministryofinspiration.com

Zander, Benjamin and Zander, Rosamund. *The Art of Possibility: Transforming Professional and Personal Life* (2000) Harvard Business Review Press http://www.benjaminzander.com

Ziglar, Zig. 'See you at the top' Simon & Schuster Audio. http://www.ziglar.com/

Recommended books

The Naked Leader and *The Naked Leader Experience* by David Taylor. Pure genius, total common sense and not a single big word

SUMO and *SUMO Your Relationships* and *How Not To Worry* by Paul McGee. Ditto! The master of simplicity continues to do what he does best

Success Intelligence by Robert Holden. I love this book. It's about small changes that have a big impact

Man's Search for Meaning by Viktor Frankl. Depressing and inspiring at the same time. A superb intro to 'logotherapy', the science of hope

The Art of Possibility, Ben and Rose Zander. I've never met the Zanders but imagine them to be as mad as a box of frogs. And incredibly entertaining and talented

Good to Great by Jim Collins. Classic business book that can be a bit hit and miss but worth buying for the hedgehog concept

Average to A+ by Alex Linley. Occasionally heavy going (in comparison with *Naked Leader* and *SUMO*, that is) but well worth the effort

Flourish by Martin Seligman. The big daddy of positive psychology writes something we can all understand. Worth reading for the first third

Bounce by Matthew Syed. A magical book that makes perfect sense

The Alchemist by Paulo Coelho. A fable. I think.

The Monk Who Sold His Ferrari by Robin Sharma. Classic self-help. Terribly cheesy but kind of satisfying

Do More Great Work by Michael Bungay Stanier. I like Michael's blogs, videos and books

The Happiness Hypothesis by Jonathan Haidt. Almost simple but not quite

Drop the Pink Elephant by Bill McFarlan. For lovers of language

Being Brilliant by Andrew Cope (sorry, couldn't help myself!). A modern fable about a circus. Actually rather good

The Happiness Advantage by Shawn Achor. Actually rather brilliant!

Oh, The Places You'll Go by Dr Seuss. Positive psychology before its time. This is the book I wish I'd written!

The Pig of Happiness by Edward Monkton. Toilet reading (takes two minutes and you'll leave inspired)

The Yes Man by Danny Wallace. Wonderful book. Terrible movie

DVDs. All have elements of positive psychology in them:

Bob the Builder box set. For those, like me, with a mental age of 7. Can we fix it?

Pay it Forward. Based on the premise of random acts of kindness. The best film in the world, ever?

The Shawshank Redemption. Great messages about the power of staying positive in adversity as well as one man's enduring power to make things happen

Little Miss Sunshine. A terrible motivational speaker and the power of influence

School of Rock. A classic movie about playing to your strengths. Plus huge energy from Jack Back!

Monsters Inc. Mike, Sully, Boo and the power of good versus evil. Unmissable!

Groundhog Day. Getting the same old s**t, day in day out? Change your approach to get a different result

Kung Fu Panda. There's no secret ingredient in the 'secret ingredient' chicken noodle soup. OMG!

Life is Beautiful. Never thought I'd be recommending an Italian film. If you want to see a 2%er in action, this movie should be top of your list

Anvil: The Story of Anvil. You won't see this on any other 'recommended movie' list. Loved it. Bouncebackability. Playing to your strengths and setting HUGGs. Oh, and plenty of heavy metal!

A Christmas Carol. Time line therapy but without the mumbo jumbo

About the authors...

Andy Cope describes himself as 'a professional trainer, qualified teacher, author and learning junkie.' He fell into retail management and then trained to be a teacher, spending 10 years cutting his teeth in adult education. Andy now runs a training company called Art of Brilliance Ltd.

He combines this with studying for a doctorate at the University of Loughborough. He used some of his research to develop a course called 'The Art of Being Brilliant' which has run to rave reviews in businesses and schools around the world.

Andy has written the best-selling children's series *Spy Dog* (published by Puffin) which won the Redhouse Children's Book of the year as well as the Richard and Judy Book Award. *Spy Dog* has sold in excess of a million copies worldwide. Andy has also written *Raccoon Rampage* for Harper Collins. He has also penned *Being Brilliant*, a self-help book for busy managers and A *Brilliant Life* and *The Game of Life*, the UK's first positive psychology books for teenagers.

Andy had never considered co-writing a book before. In fact, he wasn't sure this project would work. He was blown away by some of Andy Whittaker's ideas and he grudgingly admits that the laugh-out-loud sections of the book are all Andy W's bits. While he finds this faintly annoying, he basks in the glory that although Andy is very funny, his Morecambe schooling means he's hopeless at putting sentences together! (He's confident that his co-author doesn't know what an apostrophe is, never mind being able to spell it!)

Andy's ambition is to get positive psychology on the syllabus in every school in the land, and to be able to surf brilliantly.

Andy Cope can be contacted at andy@artofbrilliance.co.uk
His website is www.artofbrilliance.co.uk
His Twitter account is @beingbrilliant

Andy Whittaker has been described as the best thing to come out of Morecambe since the M6 motorway. He is Lancashire's answer to Anthony Robbins (great big fella from America who does an amazing job motivating people and walks on fire). Andy is also a very nice bloke.

Andy Whittaker is an NLP Trainer as well as being a bit OCD on self-development. He reads voraciously (often scurrying to a dictionary to look up the meaning of big words, like 'voraciously'!). He agrees with Andy C that all the best ideas in this book are his. But deep down he's very grateful to Andy C for helping him put the sentences in order. And those apostrophes are a real pain!

Andy is firmly rooted in the real world. He works with the other Andy. He can talk in big words but prefers not to, focusing instead on bringing his life experiences into play, connecting with people from all walks of life. He has spent time observing behaviour in companies big and small. More importantly, he has spent his time learning about leadership, communication, human interaction and goal setting. He is firmly rooted at the modern end of the personal development spectrum and is comfortable with group training or individual coaching, always drawing on his NLP skills to achieve amazing results.

Andy is an immensely likeable personality and an exceptionally funny speaker. He has that rarest of talents, the ability to take you through a real life journey of ups and downs that will connect with you, whoever you are.

Andy has a young daughter so spare time is rare. However, he does occasionally moonlight as a stand-up comedian, which is a great release from the pressures of modern life.

Andy's ambition is to be the best trainer in the world.

Andy Whittaker can be contacted at andyw@artofbrilliance.co.uk
His website is www.artofbrilliance.co.uk
His Twitter account is @artofbrillandyw

Acknowledgements

Andy Cope

Thanks to the usual suspects... Lou, Sophie and Ollie. Ma and pa. I know you think I'm mad but it always works out in the end. And a collection of people who probably don't realise how important they've been in shaping my thinking... Mickey P (good to have you back matey), Steve Kay, Jackie Rawling and the genius that is Cliff Sinclair (start believing it Cliffster).

Special mention to Kev Brown for a truly awesome quote and for demonstrating a sometimes belligerent 2% attitude! Not sure what to say about Ed Peppitt other than 'wow!' and 'thanks'.

Unbelievable gratitude to David 'Naked Leader' Taylor who's demonstrated that some gurus are truly worthy of their pedestal. And I can't leave without mentioning my 2%ers group... the maddest and most positive bunch of weirdos imaginable! As Hilda Ogden once said, 'The world is your lobster.'

And a final but massive hats off to the British educational system in the 1980s for failing Mr Andrew Whittaker. He's a very late developer (some may say we're still waiting). How poor must the schools have been to let someone out the other end with no more than a basic grasp of written English? If he'd had a decent education he wouldn't have needed my help in correcting his stuff and there would have been no book! He's a living, breathing example to kids everywhere. His message seems to be 'Reading and writing? Don't bother. Someone will do it for you!'

Andy Whittaker

Dedicated to my mum and dad (Thel and Dave) – thanks for having me!

My inspiration is taken on a daily basis from my daughter Olivia, nephew Ben and niece Sammy. Behave yourselves and work hard at school!

Thanks to my sister Bobby, brother-in-law Graham, Annie and Colin for all your support. Jim and Elan Thomas, Sally Lyons, Steve Kay, John Lievers, Charles Ford and Craig Nobby McNab for giving me my first shots at speaking in public. Acid-tongued Justin Clarkson for being a hero and the lads (you know who you are).

And to my wonderful, beautiful, intelligent, angel faced (I know you will be reading this) girlfriend Tilly. I love you with all my heart.

I have to finish with a massive thanks to Andy Cope, my co-author. Without his ability to put a comma in the right place my bits would never have made it in. Thanks mate.

The 2%ers club...

The messages in this book are simple, but not easy. Academically it's a doddle. But actually being positive and upbeat in the modern world is very challenging indeed. In short, being brilliant is easy. Staying brilliant is a lifetime challenge. So we figured it'd be easier if you had some help. Hence we've formed a 2%ers club. Think of it as a meeting of like-minded souls, all searching for brilliance, striving for excellence and with a determination to lead positive lives.

'I refuse to join any club that would have me as a member.'
Groucho Marx

We currently run two meetings a year. It gives us a chance to introduce people to the latest thinking in areas such as positive psychology, emotional intelligence, entropy and appreciative inquiry. Basically, we fill a room full of positive people and have a damned good day.

So, don't be a Groucho. If you want to sign up for the 2%ers club or would like to receive our 'occasional' blog, please log on to www.artofbrilliance.co.uk